Only Remember the Laughter

First edition
published in 2005 by

WOODFIELD PUBLISHING
Bognor Regis, West Sussex, England
www.woodfieldpublishing.com

ISBN 1-903953-77-4

Only Remember the Laughter

A PERSONAL MEMOIR

June O'Carroll Robertson

Woodfield

To the members of the
Limerick Civic Trust
with my love and gratitude

Contents

~~~~~~

Introduction

If one is lucky enough to have children, making a will should be fairly straightforward. Unless, horrible thought, they have little interest in their heritage and are hell bent on selling everything and taking off for the nearest fashionable resort.

As Jimmy and I had no children, we were faced with the heavy responsibility of finding a home for the various beautiful things that I had been fortunate to inherit. My father, Tony O'Carroll-Scott and his first cousin, Rosaleen Tausch had been born and brought up at Lissenhall, just outside Nenagh in Co Tipperary. Although their tastes differed in many ways, they were united in their deep love for the old home and their Irish roots, even though, for financial and political reasons, they had been unable to spend their adult lives there. It was their dearest wish that the remaining furniture and treasures, such as pictures, swords and medals should return to Ireland, to serve as a memorial to the family of which I am the last living descendant.

The Carrol family was an ancient one, which could trace its roots back to ancient Celtic chieftains. In spite of wars and civil wars, it was possible to follow the history of my ancestors in some detail from the end of the eighteenth century. Jimmy and I thoroughly agreed with the plan of returning the family treasures to Ireland. Apart from being responsible, Jimmy was a historian and towards the end of his life, we tried in vain to find a home for our inheritance. It was a long and difficult quest, with many disappointments along the way and, when Jimmy died, I was faced with a still unsolved problem.

Then Fate, or the ancestors, or my Guardian Angel or perhaps all three intervened and I was introduced to the Limerick Civic Trust. This introduction came about through the kind concern of Angela and Peter Swift, my very good friends who live in a manor house opposite my cottage in the village. Throughout all the legal negotiations, another friend, John Isherwood, who has been our solicitor for over thirty years, helped me. His guidance has taken away from me much of the anxiety and uncertainty of becoming a widow.

The Limerick Civic Trust had bought a charming Georgian house, number 2, Pery Square in Limerick and lovingly restored it to being a gracious home. I could not spare any furniture in my lifetime, but there were many things that I could give them straight away, including family pictures, swords, medals and all the family papers.

It has been like a happy ending to a fairy tale, for apart from finding a safe and permanent home for the family things; it has given me the pleasure of discovering new and wonderful friends. In a world where one is often faced with cynicism and self-interest, it has been a joy to meet with sincerity and kindness in the members of the Trust. They are remarkable in their dedication and their sensitivity to the feelings of others, and I can never be sufficiently grateful to them all.

After the opening of the collection by the British Ambassador in November 2002, Denis Leonard asked me if I would record my own life to complete the family history and, in the following pages, I have tried to do just that. This in itself has brought me in touch with other new and delightful friends. Group Captain David Greenwood recorded my dictation for me, Debbie Jacobs transcribed his tapes and Marjorie Quarton, who helped me with my first book *A Long Way from Tipperary,* advised me to write this introduction. I owe them all a great debt of gratitude.

It has sometimes been painful to recall some of these memories, but now I prefer to remember only the laughter. I hope my readers will do the same.

Acknowledgements

~~~~~~

These memoirs would never have been published without the help of a number of very kind friends.

Pamela Mills has been a dear friend for many years and I was so happy to have her charming drawings to illustrate my second book. I am very grateful to the Limerick Civic Trust for asking me to complete the saga of my father's Irish family by recounting the story of my own life and, most of all, for giving such a gracious and caring home to the family treasures.

I would also like to thank David Greenway who recorded my first scribbled draft, corrected my abysmal spelling and made those sessions such fun. I shall always remember his kindness the first time we met when he disentangled my duvet cover which had tied itself into a Gordian knot in my washing machine!

This whole venture has introduced me to new friends and I am so happy to have the friendship of Debbie Jacob of the Limerick Civic Trust. She went to unending trouble in transcribing David's tapes onto computer disks for me.

Ten years ago, Marjorie Quarton guided me through my first book "A Long Way From Tipperary" and she has been a close friend ever since. Now once again she has set me on course and taken away so much of the hassle and anxiety of launching a book. She has all my loving gratitude.

My cousin David Gwynne-James has never failed to give us support and encouragement and, since Jimmy died, I have been especially grateful for all his love and thoughtfulness.

Finally, I would like to thank all my very special friends in Penton Mewsey. Angela and Peter Swift first introduced me to the Limerick

Civic Trust and they helped me so much in entertaining the members when they came to visit me.

John Isherwood has been our wonderful friend and counsellor for many years. He has been, and is, a true lifeline, sorting out my problems and always giving me wise advice. I shall be forever in his debt.

Finally, I have to thank Geoff Townson for all his kindness and expertise. Geoff is a very near neighbour and with his computer knowledge he has taken on all my technical problems and even persuaded me that T stands for Tango not Tommy!

And I can never forget the dear friends who take Sophie for nose-sniffing walks. Jenny and Bob Goddard and Carol Webber keep Sophie slim and shining when I'm caught at my desk and they make us both very happy.

CHAPTER ONE

A Victorian Childhood

~~~~~~

The white rabbit put on his spectacles.
'Where shall I begin please Your Majesty?' he asked.
'Begin at the beginning', the King said very gravely,
'And go on until you come to the end, then stop'.

The King was right. My permanently overworked guardian angel must have had quite a job on his hands to assist me into this world. In 1928, pre natal care was almost unknown, mothers and their babies were not tested and monitored and the fact that I arrived intact was a case of good luck, a lot of suffering and little judgement as far as I can tell. My mother was small boned and very frightened and she was about to have a seven and a half pound baby when a five-pound infant would have been more than enough for her. She was in labour for two days, while the two doctors made soothing noises and discussed garden birds with my father and grandfather. Fortunately my guardian angel had granny on his side; she had borne eight children including two sets of twins and although she would worry and fuss over trifles she was a tower of strength in an emergency.

In her devotion to children she worked for fifty years as secretary to the Waifs and Strays Society in Hereford and many mothers gave her their ailing children to nurse back to health when they lost confidence in their doctors' treatment. I think my father was more grateful to granny than to the two doctors who eventually brought me out into the sunlight on a May morning with the help of horrible instruments of torture. After my arrival, my father made up his mind that my mother would never again have to go through such an experience and for that reason I grew up as an only child.

I was born in my grandparents' house in Hereford, but my first conscious memory was that of being carried into the children's ward of Salisbury Hospital when I was three. My poor parents must have

1929 My father and I at Coombe Beach, North Cornwall – my first sight of the sea

1928 Drawing of Aylestone Hill, Hereford – where I was born

been through a wretchedly anxious time, for three doctors had failed to find the problem. Then an elderly country doctor recalled that he had had another patient just like me. That patient had been treated and recovered and so did I.

When I was seven I went to live with my grandparents. My father was in the army and in 1936 he was posted to India. My mother was to follow him, but my childhood illness prevented me accompanying them. Little did any of us imagine at that first parting that we should only be together for two and a half months in the next nine years! However, I was a fortunate child, because I was left with my much loved maternal grandparents, my kindly governess, Jeff, and a host of loving aunts and uncles.

The family home, which had been planned by my grandfather for his growing family, was built in the Gothic style. It was the first house to be built on Aylestone Hill overlooking the ancient city of Hereford. I remember that the high windows faced south overlooking a sweeping lawn, beautiful trees and a distant view of the Black Mountains. I could not tell you the number of rooms in the old home, but the family all fitted in somewhere besides its share of visitors. The top floor was home for the six indoor staff. Granny was a Vicar's daughter, and although she had the blood of John of Gaunt in her veins, she would have considered a butler inappropriate. She ruled the house with the help of two parlour maids, two housemaids, a formidable cook, Mrs Dowling and a subdued kitchen maid. Granny was single minded and she overcame most of life's difficulties with the ominous phrase, 'You know I'm right, dear.'

Essentially, she was deeply religious and truly loving, but faced with a large and devoted family, there were sometime dramatic blowups, which had to be soothed and settled by Auntie Mamie, her eldest child and an equally loving Governess called Semming. My mother told me that once when she was small she knelt to say her evening prayers at what she took to be Semming's knees. She murmured with head bent and closed eyes, 'Please God let there be no fusses and rows'. Granny's knees went rigid with indignation and my mother's prayer was not answered.

As a young and beautiful girl, my grandmother had broken off her engagement to her titled fiancée, 'Because he drank, dear'. Shortly after this, my grandfather sat behind her in church and fell in love with her beautiful hair, which tumbled down her back red gold like a lion's mane. It was the beginning of a very happy marriage in which they comforted and supported each other for over fifty years. Granny was always suspicious of alcohol. Grandpa was abstemious, but he kept an excellent cellar for his guests. A wise doctor had once recommended that granny should have a glass of Emu Port with her lunch to guard against anaemia. The glass of port became part of the luncheon ritual, but she liked to remind the family that she only took it on doctor's orders. My grandmother always carved and, to my consternation, she invariably spooned some of the gory juices of the joint over my plate. 'It's good for you dear'. I had been brought up not to complain but to this day I prefer my meat very well cooked. Grandpa also had his problems. He regularly passed his plate back to granny with the words, 'You've given me too much, Sunny.' She would nod in agreement, rearrange his helping, and return it. He always ate it.

Grandpa's sisters were notable hostesses in Edwardian society and I'm sure their menus were worthy of their butlers, but when they stayed with my grandparents they must have come down to earth with a bump. Granny's catering was essentially nursery fare; delicious and beautifully cooked, but very simple. Paté de foie gras never crossed the threshold, but the family was fond of 'hasty pudding' or 'thunder and lightning', which consisted of plain sweet cornflour made with milk and a large spoonful of golden syrup. Sometimes I was allowed to write my name in syrup as a special treat.

This basic fare may have been owing to the fact that my great-grandfather was a saint. Saintliness is a wonderful quality but when it resulted in my great-grandfather regularly giving away his lunch to the first tramp to knock on the vicarage door, he must have made my great-grandmother's housekeeping rather complicated. I clearly remember my Sunday morning breakfasts with my grandfather and governess. The silver dishes were always laid out on a brass trivet in front of a blazing fire and we had what grandpa called 'Indian breakfast.' This was plain boiled rice, sausages and a boiled egg broken up over the top, mixed into a gooey mess. For many years, I imagined haughty Indian Maharajahs enjoying the same treat.

Granny was a true missionary and she had dragooned all her family into happily accepting the Christian faith, but once they'd all grown up I was her only captive disciple. Sundays were as regular and as constant as the seasons but they included plenty of action. After Indian breakfast we got ready for church and, because of the number of garments we were compelled to wear, this took some time. Although there were fires in all the rooms and sometimes in the bedroom I shared with my governess, there were many icy corners in the old house. So I was probably glad of my woollen combinations, my woollen vest, my liberty bodice, my woollen jumper, and tweed skirt. For church, this was topped up with gaiters (I forget how many buttons they had but it seemed an awful lot), a tweed overcoat and a felt hat secured with elastic under the chin.

I don't think I was a pretty child but I always felt that my family could have made more of me. My hair was red gold like granny's, but it was dead straight and instead of accepting defeat and leaving it straight, with a snood like Alice, I was given two alternatives, two insignificant plaits or curls on Sundays. The curls were achieved with the use of rags, which were used to roll up the hair and tied in a bump on my scalp. This made sleeping uncomfortable and after all the suffering the curls quietly disentangled themselves at the first hint of rain or fog. One rather sadistic great aunt used to give me an extra rag bump on the top of my head, 'Just like Topsy dear, so amusing'. I look back now at some of these early snaps showing a gawky freckled child with plaits, wearing a velvet dress with a lace

Around 1935 - I had curls on Sunday

collar and boy's stockings. How could they! Fortunately, I was not encouraged to look in the mirror.

But to return to Sunday; my grandparents, my governess, Jeff, and I were driven to church by my mother's youngest sister Trill. In spite of several proposals she never married but lived at home and was therefore able to drive grandpa about the county to see his clients. Besides being a much loved family solicitor he was also Under Sheriff, a former Mayor of Hereford, a Registrar of Hereford County Court and the Legal Secretary to the Bishop. Seated between my grandparents in church there was no opportunity to be anything but outwardly pious although I recall gazing admiringly at the second choirboy on the right. After church the ancient upright Austin car took us safely home to where granny would continue the Vicar's work with a lesson on my catechism and a long and incredibly heavy going tale from a book called *Stories from the Collects*. The children in these stories took several pages before they saw the error of their ways and became good. I'm sure granny found it all very tiring but we soldiered on together until the gong rang for lunch.

Lunch was usually roast beef and Yorkshire pudding and apple pie and cream, but after lunch came my big treat of the day, a walk with grandpa. 'Where are you going, Frank?' enquired granny and grandpa would show one of his rare displays of rebellion, 'Picking poppies on the moon, Sunny.' My grandfather was probably the plainest member of the family but he was certainly the dearest. His only brother was a judge and such a very good-looking judge that Millais had used him as a model in his youth. His three sisters were all beautiful, formidable possibly, but also graceful and elegant in a way that seems to have been lost since Edwardian times. Grandpa was a little shorter than Granny and a long walrus moustache hid part of his kind face, but he had beautiful, sensitive, long fingered hands, which he had inherited from his father.

Grandpa and I had two kinds of walk. The ones I enjoyed the most were country walks for he was a knowledgeable countryman with a passion for birds and trees and every kind of wild life. Grandpa loved all trees and the family was considerably astonished when he ordered the felling of three beautiful elms, which grew in the garden overhanging the road. 'They're beautiful, Taffy', he explained to me, 'But they are dangerous, they have shallow roots'. Now I wonder if he was describing trees or people. Side by side my grandfather and I would wander through the woods and fields and if our rambles took us up a little hill, we would stop and admire the view, because I'd been told that grandpa had a bad heart. I'd been born on his birthday and when I was eight he was eighty.

Sometimes, to my acute embarrassment, our walks took us into other people's gardens. My grandfather had a special love for oaks and holly trees and if he spotted a tiny sapling in a neighbour's garden, he had no hesitation in walking in and digging it up. 'They don't want it, Taffy' he'd say. He always called me Taffy after Kipling's Taffimai, which means, 'small person without any manners who ought to be spanked.' I found it very hard to believe the owners of the saplings did not want them, so I would stand between grandpa and the over-looking windows of the house with my skirts held out to hide this fearful act of felony. I think the small oaks and holly trees probably did far better under grandpa's care and he was certainly most generous

Around 1935 - Disgraceful felony!

with his wood. His friends and family were given beautiful polished holly walking sticks and the dining room in the Green Dragon Hotel in Hereford was panelled entirely from grandpa's oak trees.

Sometimes, grandpa would take me on an urban walk to look at some of the new housing in Hereford in which he was deeply interested. Being a fair and compassionate man, he wanted all his fellow citizens to have well built, airy houses with bathrooms and good sanitation, but I remember him saying to me, 'Well they have a bathroom in their new home Taffy, but they only use it to keep the coal in'. On these town excursions, we occasionally met a Walls ice-cream man peddling his wares around the streets ringing his bicycle bell to alert his customers. Grandpa would halt the man with his raised thumb-stick and buy me an ice cream with a whole packet of wafers, which he handed to me one by one. It was rather like having a mid-night feast, delicious exciting and dangerous, for such outrageous behaviour would have been strictly forbidden by granny.

After our afternoon ramble, grandpa and I would return home for drawing room tea, which included chocolate cake, my favourite, sultana cake, grandpa's favourite and caraway seed, granny's favourite. There was always an extra guest for Sunday afternoon tea. Maud Bull had played with grandpa when they were both small children. She was highly intellectual but she was quite the plainest woman in England and therefore no possible danger to granny. No speck of powder had ever dusted her face, her complexion was the colour and texture of window putty, and she had an unfortunate wart on her chin. But the James family was always kind and, over the years, she had been adopted as kind of a family mascot. In the days before the First World War, she had a positive crush on the German Kaiser, so much so that she had a coat and skirt tailored for herself, which was an exact replica of a German officer's uniform, complete with a hat with a dashing cockade. She always had a very smart pony and trap, which she drove with considerable flourish and a diminutive dachshund named Fritz.

When the First War broke out granny and grandpa like so many of their friends, lost one of the dearest of their children. Uncle Eric was given the DSO for rescuing a wounded man in a wheelbarrow from a particularly hellish part of that terrible shell ridden trench landscape. But he was to die of wounds soon afterwards. He'd been a great friend of the Arkwright family and I always feel Sir John Arkwright was thinking of him and his contemporaries when he wrote the hymn, *Oh Valiant Hearts*.

Poor Maud Bull, she still kept her pony and trap and her little dog but her brave German uniform was put away forever and she continued to come to tea. She must have starved herself the week before, because she always managed to fit in two tea parties on a Sunday. Her first call was at the Bishop's Palace and her next at Aylestone Hill. I can still hear her say, 'Yes I would like that cake after I've had this one.' After Sunday tea it was back to duty again and I had to write my weekly letter to my parents in India. I discovered the following letter written in December 1936 amongst the papers.

December 20

> *Darling Mummie and Daddy*
> *Thank you so much for the lovly letters you both sent me they were interesting all about the Indians and how they they thik about Xmas when those Sekh are so they must have hair as long as a mile I hope if any body opens this they wont read this because if they were a Sikh they mite be rather cross the other day I was in Greenlands and wanted to get Jeff her birthday present so I told her to go away and look at the toys and she did then I went up to an assistant how had served us the day befor and how was the nicest in the shop and I asked her what Jeff would like and at that she caled to anenther assistant 'perfume don't you think' and there was I not noing in the least what perfume was then she brought a batool of perfume and I understand that it was scent and I said I had only a shilling so she said I could have it*

for that and I had to hope for the best about the smell and I wondered
wy she said she would let me have it for a shiling and it was not till
a few days after that that I was looking at the box when I saw that
it had got 1/3 on it wasent it kind of her she had let me have it for a
shiling and I am going to thank her when I go down there again and
at last this morning I gave it her she loved it and I was glad I gave
it her because it was eau de colgne and she had just run short. Last
night I nealy exploded with serprise because a card came from Uncle
Henry of a pitcher of his ship and a pound note from the bank of
England so now I am well away yesterday Granie gave us a calender
it is of London and they send one evry year and the last one the sent
is a Windsar and is in the lavatry!! Jeff and I have just been discusing
how we are to address the anvelope to and she siad wy not to them
both but I said no because they might think Mummie was in the army
and they would think she was a Russian and I don't like those people
much becaus they are so bolshie don't you think so I think I must say
Au revior at last till my next letter best love

Your very loving

June

XOXOX
XXX

My governess was obviously an early follower of the 'don't worry
about spelling as long as they express themselves' philosophy. This
resulted in my lifetime struggle with spelling and when many years
later I taught small children, I put correct spelling fairly high on the
curriculum.

Those far off Sundays finally ended with hymns with granny at the
piano. Granny was a good musical all-rounder and she was proficient
at the piano, the organ, the accordion, the concertina and the cello.
We played and sang all the old favourites and we never blanched at
that verse in *All Things Bright and Beautiful*.

The rich man in his castle,
The poor man at his gate,
He made them high and lowly,
And ordered their estate…

It was the accepted order of things in those days and it took another World War to turn things on their heads and bring about a social revolution. I shall always wonder what demon of mischief came over me the day I remarked, 'Of course granny, it doesn't make any difference to me whether I sing hymns or not!' Oh horrors, oh calamity, if Granny had been an avenging angel, she could have not been more angry. I was in disgrace for a whole week, but at the end of the week she forgave me and gave me a present. She always did that after some imperial rocket, and of course, I was quite wrong, it did make a difference. Learning about our Lord, learning to love our Lord, may have been tough going at times but how wonderful to know that one was always loved, one was never alone. What better armour for life.

My grandmother was undoubtedly very good but just occasionally she would prove that she too was entirely human and she could be really bad too. These bursts of wickedness occurred when grandpa was away on official duties. He'd obviously ignored her pleas that he knew she was right, and while he was out of the house, she had the telephone installed. Time passed, her sin was forgiven, and grandpa was rash enough to go away again. This time she had lightning conductors erected on the house. She may have been right because the house did stand on the top of a hill, but granny's worst crime, which must have taken all grandpa's love to forgive was when she ordered all his white fan tailed pigeons to be shot.

As a small child, I loved to hear their gentle cooing and watch them alight on the greenhouse roof like a host of snowy angels. Admittedly over the years, some of them had intermingled with the pigeons from the Bishop's Palace. These pigeons were grey and rather insignificant, so some of the angels were not as white as they should be. I do not think that granny was concerned with their colour, but she was highly indignant when they invaded some of the bedrooms and left messes all over the occupants' dressing tables. Grandpa was not concerned with such details and he departed on a business trip with no suspicion of what was to come. Pritchard the gardener, my special friend, was ordered to do the dreadful deed and it all seemed the more horrible because he appeared with his shotgun early one morning wearing his bowler hat. The noise of shotgun fire would have done credit to a gathering on a Scottish moor on 12 August. It was really horrendous to see the dying birds falling all over the garden and greenhouse roof, their white plumage stained with their own blood like the massacre of the Huguenots. What dreadful bedroom scene took place on grandpa's return, I shall never know. Perhaps granny admitted that she had been really, truly bad. At any rate, I cannot remember her ever being wicked again and as she grew older and life became harder, she grew in gentleness and sweetness. However much she suffered with bad health and financial worries she never complained.

Apart from teaching me my catechism, granny also instructed me that having anything to do with boys was bad. My father, grandfather and uncles were naturally exonerated, but boys in general were to be avoided unless of course one was lucky enough to meet 'Mr. Right'. If one happy day Mr. Right appeared, than her solution was – leave them alone together dear! She did not stipulate how long for. Although she had borne, eight children she did not consider it was her task to give her daughters or granddaughters any kind of sex education.

When my Aunt Grace, who had married my mother's twin brother, Uncle Pip, was expecting her first baby, she confided her wonderful secret to me. I was proud and overwhelmed to be able to share in the excitement of this miraculous event to come. But granny never mentioned anything about babies to come, she merely said, 'Auntie Grace has been having headaches dear, she must rest.' Unfortunately, not long after this my Aunt Trill had a real headache probably partly a hangover after dancing the night away at a series of hunt balls. So, when I was told that I must be quiet because Auntie Trill had a headache I shattered the household by exclaiming, 'Oh is she going to have a baby too?'

I'm sure my grandfather would not have worried if I had seen him in his dressing gown, but my grandmother was determined he should not suffer any embarrassment. She would rustle ahead of him, her beautiful long white hair floating about her shoulders and exclaim, 'Don't come out dears, your grandfather is going to have a bath.' Aylestone Hill had two bathrooms, I seem to recall that sometimes the housemaids would carry a small hip bath into the guest rooms and fill it from cans of scalding hot water. The cold water always stood in a jug on the washstand in each bedroom. The bathroom which was used by my aunt and various uncles, Jeff, my governess and me, was rather more modern, for the bath stood robustly on four sturdy legs and you just turned the taps to receive hot and cold water. My grandparent's bathroom was dark and more mysterious. The bath was encased in a mahogany surround and was filled by an extremely temperamental geyser, which was liable to hiss scalding steam, like some angry dragon. To complete the picture, over the bath there hung a stuffed alligator. Where this highly unsuitable gift had come from I never discovered. It may be that my grandfather was fond of it, but it did not encourage me to linger in the bath, on the rare occasions when I used my grandparent's bathroom.

The early years of my childhood were restricted by the awful possibility that I might catch something and my former illness might reoccur. In consequence, I rarely played with other children and I was never allowed to go into Woolworths. I would imagine that the congregation of St. Peters was just as liable to pass on infection, but in granny's eyes, Woolworths was a positive cauldron of germs. She also told me that I must never eat a green sweet, because one of my uncles died from eating a green sweet. I eventually discovered that after swallowing the green sweet he had fallen out of a window.

Occasionally, if the city was reasonably clear of epidemics, I was allowed to visit Guerneys, the grocer, which had an intriguing overhead tram system for taking your money and returning the change. Having bought a packet of tea or half a pound of bacon sliced at number four, the assistant would receive your money and place it in an overhanging tube. She would then pull a handle and the tube would go sailing away over our heads to be received by an accountant who sat high up in a glass-fronted box. The accountant would then extract the half crown (such a delightful well worth having coin) place the change back in the tube and back it would come, weaving its way over our heads to be returned to our purse. I would happily stand forever watching these little tubes criss-crossing their way across the shop. It was almost as good as a visit to the station.

The chemist was memorable for those vast bottles of coloured liquid, which stood in the window – red and green, amber and blue. They cheered the grey street until the lamp lighter came around with his ladder to turn up the gas on the street lamps. Another treat was a visit to the shoe shop. Having tried on what the family considered to be a thoroughly practical shoe, one was encouraged to walk up two steps to the X-ray machine. This machine had three viewing holes, one for myself, where I could see the blue skeleton of my foot wriggling away, proving there was plenty of room for my toes, one for Jeff, who had to persuade herself there was plenty of room for me to grow and one for the shop assistant, who with great authority, gave the last word on the complete suitability of the chosen shoe.

One day, Jeff and I noticed that a small crowd had gathered outside the window of Edward's the drapers. Had Edward's imported some new fashion from Paris, we wondered? But no, the assembled onlookers were gazing awestruck at the window itself, which was not vertical so that one could admire one's own reflection, but curved inwards in a great arc, which gave the effect of making the glass invisible. It was all very new and modern but perhaps a little dull, when one could not see if one's hat was straight.

My childhood may have lacked the company of other children, but it taught me from an early age to be content in my own company. In those days of childish innocence, to compensate for my lack of children to play with, I peopled my small world with fairies. I read all the fairytales I was lucky enough to be given, the tales in which the princess was always rescued by her prince and lived happily ever after, having endured countless hardships, cruelties and rescues from dragons. I was a hopeless romantic and I shunned caricature and insisted on happy endings. So Hans Anderson with his tragic little mermaid was not one of my favourites.

Aylestone Hill had a fairly big garden – vast to a small child, and one of my favourite trees was a tall very beautiful copper beech. Some of the lower branches grew close to the ground. Although I was not naturally adventurous, I was able to climb up and settle myself comfortably into my own private house. The rain sometimes collected in a small channel between the branches and so quite naturally, I was able to have my very own sink. But my passionate belief in fairies sometimes encouraged me to write little notes and leave them small bunches of flowers. Fortunately, I had two loyal friends who never betrayed me and very occasionally replied with a suitable note written in very small writing and signed the Fairy Queen.

My days would have been much lonelier if it hadn't have been for the companionship of Pritchard and Ankers. Pritchard was a full time gardener, short and stocky with a round kindly face and twinkling blue eyes. Ankers taller, leaner but equally kind, combined the tasks of mowing the lawns, driving grandpa to the office in his chauffeur's uniform and at times acting as a groom to Trill's horse. They were my friends and confidantes and I must have wasted hours of their time. On rare occasions, I would sit with them in the saddle room in the stable yard, while they ate their lunch. I cannot remember if they drank a thermos of tea but I recall their great doorsteps of bread and cheese. The saddle room was delectable, smelling of saddle soap and potting fibre and gun oil and tobacco and all good honest earthy things. But these visits had to be made surreptitiously because if I was spotted by granny from an upstairs window she would knock the windowpane sharply and call out 'Don't delay the men, dear!' From an early age, I came to know the meaning of the vital word 'tact'.

My mother's eldest brother was charming and amusing but he also had a gift for turning granny around his little finger with dire financial results. Being granny's favourite he also got away with some stories at the lunch table, which mummy's other brothers would never have dared to contemplate. I remember sitting round-eyed and astonished when in the middle of tomato soup he decided to recount a tale about a vicar and a parrot. He may have banked on the fact that grandpa was a little deaf. He may have prided himself that granny would accept anything he told her but the story ended with the parrot uttering the word 'bugger'! I knew instantly that was a really terrible word, judging by the fuss and the faces at the lunch table. Of course, I had no idea of its meaning but it was obviously something bad and shocking and astonishing. And so I was like the barber in the old Greek fairy tale who was so full of his dreadful secret that he had to confide to the rushes that grew along the riverbank. I too had to have my confidantes and I repeated the dreadful story to Pritchard and Ankers. I'm sure they must have found it very difficult to keep a straight face.

I was born with a fairly active conscience but, like most children, there came a day when my conscience was overturned and instincts of envy and greed took charge. I'd been to a rather dull Christmas party. It should not have been dull because any children's party was quite an event. But this one was not very exciting and half way through, a rather emaciated Father Christmas appeared to give out some presents. Some minutes after Father Christmas had disappeared our host reappeared and the scales fell from my eyes. He was covered in cotton wool. I think I realised that it would hurt my loving family as much as me if I confided to them that I knew the truth and so for at least a year afterwards we all kept up a happy game of pretence. Whether it was this loss of innocence that tipped the balance I do not know, but at the end of the afternoon when I was left alone with my co-hosts Christopher and Elizabeth, they took me to see their model farm.

At first glance, it resembled my own. They had a farmer, I had an identical farmer, they had a house, I had a similar house, they had a cow and I had a cow. They had a pig, I had a pig, but than I saw it. They had something that I did not have. I had a hen, which stood up, but they had a hen sitting on its nest laying an egg. I thought if only I could have a hen like that, I would be happy forever and ever. While Christopher and Elizabeth were admiring their barn, the hen found its way into the pocket of my green velvet party dress. It was very small but it nearly burnt a hole in my pocket. It certainly didn't make me happy. I was utterly miserable, for I could not enjoy it. I couldn't send it back and I imagined Christopher and Elizabeth searching their nursery for their lost treasure. I hated the poor hen, and myself even more. Years later I was able to tell this sad story to the children in my class and it never failed to impress them, although the odd thing continued to disappear from the classroom.

The days of my childhood were placid and secure and really wonderfully happy. I cannot remember any really dramatic event disturbing the tranquillity of the comforting routine, apart from the night when I alerted the household to a fire in one of the chimneys. Granny would move Jeff and me to sleep at the top of the house in summer because she thought it would be cooler for us. One evening shortly after being put to bed, I suddenly became aware that there was smoke curling up through the floorboards and around the bell pull. I do not think it occurred to me that the house was on fire, but it seemed an unnatural phenomenon and so I alerted the household. Shortly afterwards the fire brigade discovered a jackdaw's nest had fallen down the chimney leading to the parlour maid's pantry. The heat from the gas fire in the pantry had set the nest and the chimney fiercely alight. So it was as well that the light from the still sunny garden stole through the drawn curtains of my bedroom and kept me awake.

Twice a year my grandfather took a holiday from his office and the family set off for North Cornwall to spend some weeks in a small, thatched, utterly enchanting little house, which grandpa had started to build as a holiday home in June 1914. Tidnacott nestled against a cliff at the head of a lovely valley, which fell away to the steep cliffs above the sea. I have always loved the sea but the north coast of Cornwall seemed to be unique in its awesome grandeur. Here there are no gentle wavelets but Atlantic breakers that cast themselves on the jagged rocks and pebbles with furious primeval energy, throwing up the white spray in an angry cloud before retreating to return with renewed strength. That coast has claimed many ships and many lives and one of the most poignant memorials in Morwenstow's church-yard is a figurehead from a wrecked ship. The Rev. William Hawker erected it to mark the graves of so many drowned sailors.

Setting off for Cornwall was a momentous occasion. But whether it was a spring holiday when the valley was dotted with primroses and wild daffodils or a summer holiday, sweet with the scent of hon-eysuckle and wild roses, the cliffs dotted with cushions of sea pinks, or later the fresh clear male scent of bracken and heather, which purpled the cliffs like an emperor's robe, it was all breathtakingly beautiful. The only tragic sound, which frequently overshadowed

Around 1935 – Cuddly and Edward at Tidnacott, North Cornwall

this arcadia, was the dying scream of some wretched rabbit, which had been caught in a snare. Nature can be ruthless and cruel but it seldom causes a victim prolonged pain.

The journey from Hereford to Cornwall took some eight hours, allowing for stops, and our departure was invariably delayed because granny insisted on washing her hair and oiling her knitting machine. We would have a magnificent picnic lunch beside the roadside, but to me the most exciting stop was to have tea in Exeter. Here my grandparents, my aunt, Jeff and I would have high tea. We would have poached eggs in an extremely respectable tearoom. A small stage decorated with potted palms overlooked the crowded dining tables and three earnest ladies made up a small orchestra and entertained us with *In a Monastery Garden* and *Smoke Gets in Your Eyes*.

Granny's family, the Martyns of Tonacombe, had given grandpa this precious piece of land. Although their charming little 14th century manor house had boasted a great hall and a minstrel's gallery it must have stretched the bedrooms situation when granny returned to her old home with grandpa, eight children and all their attendants. Tonacombe was reached by a gated road, which led up through the fields and the adjoining farmyard. When I took Jimmy to Tonacombe some fifty years later, he was sure I'd have forgotten the way, knowing that my sense of locality was abysmal, but I could never forget that road and the thrill of being allowed to stand on the running board of the car so that I could spring off and open the gates.

CHAPTER TWO

Unwillingly to School

~~~~~~

Surrounded by beautiful things in my childhood, I was unaware of the hurts and anxieties, the cruelties and harsh realities that existed beyond the gates of those two beloved homes. But 1938 brought great change. Nobody told me that there were family worries; nobody told me that this safe protected existence was coming to an end. I knew the family was eagerly looking forward to my parent's return from India, but this didn't explain the worried looks, the whispered conversations which broke off abruptly when I was within earshot. Nobody spoke of the menacing clouds of war which were gathering over Europe.

I remember three incidents which brought us face to face with the full horror and reality of war. That day during the Battle of Britain when we watched two fighters collide and blow up in a ball of flame, high up in a blue cloudless sky. Whether they both belonged to us or whether one was a German aircraft, we never discovered. And the day I had to rewash a whole line of washing, because one of our bombers had limped home to base over our garden, scattering fuel from his damaged fuel tank. Then there was the never to be forgotten, awful day when I happened to be with Auntie Church when she was handed that ominous brown envelope containing the telegram telling her that her only son had been killed in his tank in the North African desert.

Auntie and Uncle Church (who were no relation of mine) lived in a thatched cottage overlooking the river at the bottom of our lane. He worked on the railway and was our village gravedigger. They were simple, kindly country people and I loved to go round and see them and have a cookery lesson. Bill, their only child had been a gentle shy young man and I remembered seeing him on his last leave, sitting on an upturned bucket in their porch shelling peas and smiling up at me in the sunshine. I knew I was helpless to comfort her so I fled to find Jeff.

Fortunately, I was shielded from knowledge of the brutality of the fighting in the Far East, but I recall begging God to let my father be killed rather than taken prisoner by the Japanese. But I am looking ahead. The War years were still to come. First came the reunion with my parents.

I was taken up to London to meet my parents at Victoria Station and seeing my mother running down the platform to greet me I opened my arms wide, closing them around not only her neck, but a neck of a charming but astonished Indian gentleman who happened to be walking alongside of her. My father and my governess had to unlock us and I was forgiven but I sometimes wonder if that kindly man looked back with amusement at his rapturous reception.

That first night of their return home, Aunt Trill told my parents about the horrendous family crisis. Trill, like so many of us, was a complicated mixture. At her best, she was brave, talented and wonderful with children. But there was a thread of self-pity and spitefulness in her nature and she delighted in spreading bad news. It must have been a terrible shock for my parents to discover that the old house was to be sold and my grandparents would have to move into a far smaller semi-detached house in Hereford. There had been family worries and grandpa had invested unwisely. Granny had been unaware of the appalling over-draft until the crisis broke, but now the truth had to be faced and the sale was being planned. It must have been the worst possible time for any sale, for who would then want to take on a large labour intensive house? So many beautiful things, like the pair of Stubbs pictures of mares with their foals, were knocked down for a few pounds when they would have brought in many thousands of pounds later on. I was whisked away from all this drama, but as I grew older I realised that my grandparents had faced up to this calamity with great courage and resolution. My mother's twin brother Uncle Pip undertook to pay off the fearsome over-draft and keep the family firm of solicitors going.

My father was a highly professional soldier, just returned from India where he had spent his leaves sailing, riding, climbing the lower slopes of the Himalayas after ibex and pursuing his great-est love, falconry. On his return home, he was faced with a major decision. What was to be done with his only child? My future had been planned long before. At the age of ten I was to go to a small exclusive boarding school run by Uncle Rowland's highly intelligent sisters. I would have had my own room and a pale blue uniform and I would have spent the holidays with my grandparents at Aylestone Hill until my parent's return two years later. But now there would be no Aylestone Hill and my holidays would be spent with ageing grandparents in a small, restricted household.

My father was decisive but ruthless and, looking back, perhaps a little insensitive. He'd always respected granny and had been grateful to her and he was devoted to grandpa with whom he'd had so much in common, but now his ears went back. He visualised me becom-ing even more 'churchy' and suburban, while he had dreams of a daughter who would be happiest halfway down a fox's earth His Irish blood was up and he wanted independence from Mummy's family. I was to mix with his mother's old friends who dreamed of horses and hunting, rather than with respectable members of granny's Mother's Union. With this in mind, my governess was invited to become my legal guardian and we would live in our own small house in Bedford where I would attend the High School as a daygirl. D had the best intentions, and he did not want me to be a further burden to my grandparents, but he completely over-looked Auntie Mamie and Uncle Rowland, who had no children of their own, who had always loved me and would have given me a gracious, cultured, loving home. The trouble was that Uncle Rowland was a clergyman and my father, who was a sincere Christian, had 'a thing' about priests.

Uncle Rowland was married to Auntie Mamie, Mummy's eldest sister. They lived in a beautiful old Queen Ann rectory just outside Hereford. As his stipend from running three country parishes amounted to just £200 a year, they certainly could have not existed if Uncle Rowland had not been astute with his money. Since a young man working in London, he had bought and sold lovely pictures and furniture and rare books and china, so that you nodded to a Romney or a Lely in the drawing room, brushed past a possible Rubens on the staircase and discovered a minor Gainsborough in a passage leading to the kitchen. His library contained first editions of all the 'coloured' fairy books, as well as an amazing collection of all the classics, for Uncle Rowland was a scholar as well as a very much loved clergyman, an art dealer and a perfect darling.

Auntie Mamie was equally loveable and highly intelligent. She had been a theatre sister in the First World War, she'd studied the piano in Germany under a pupil of Liszt and with her knowledge of German she had coached Uncle Henry into the Navy. She was also a keen gardener and botanist. So my beloved father made one of the worst decisions of his life. But perhaps it was a lucky accident and it may have all turned out for the best in the end. If I had been cared for by Auntie Mamie and Uncle Rowland, I'm sure I would have learnt much of beauty, culture and taste but I would not have come to know the other side of life or seen home backgrounds quite different from my own. I would have been too sheltered and it was time I woke up to reality.

My father's leave was curtailed and he had to return to India after barely two months, because he'd been appointed an instructor at the Staff College in Quetta. My mother was to follow him a few weeks later but she just had time to settle Jeff and myself and our old yellow

Labrador, Vulcan, into our new home. Vulcan had spent the previous three years with one of my father's brother officers, but now he had returned home. Although I have loved and lived with Labradors all my life, and loved each one of them devotedly, I remember Vulcan as a special gold link in a precious chain.

Our small semi-detached house in a crescent in Bedford was compact and pleasant and my parents had furnished it with furniture that had been stored for some years. This included some of the furniture that had come to Daddy from Lissenhall, his old Irish home, when his mother died. So my great-great grandfather watched over my homework in the dining room and the elegant little Regency chaise longue had a place in the minute drawing room.

My first day at school was the 21 September 1938 and even now in my old age I look back on that unforgettable day as the day that I discovered hell existed. I cannot blame the school, I'm sure they tried hard and taught me much, but the cultural shock of never having mixed with other children and being sent to a school of 600 girls was horrendous. The noise, the in-fighting, the pettiness of small girls was overwhelming. My family had taught me to think of others and always take the smallest slice of cake, but now I understood that to survive at school one had to have a certain knowledge of jungle warfare.

My mother was intensely loving and she looked back on her own school days as some of the happiest in her life, but over the years she had apparently forgotten the psychology she must have needed to become head girl and head of games at St George's, Ascot. Her first mistake was over my school uniform. I'm sure the High School must have pondered long in their search to find the most unflattering uniform they could devise. I imagine this was done not out of malice but with one intent – on no account must the girls appear attractive to boys. To be fair, our dark blue skirts and cardigans, white blouses and school ties were plain but passable; but the ultimate horror was our school hat. Oh how I wished we could have worn boaters. A boater can make even the plainest girl reasonably pretty but we were ordered to have a shapeless, semi-brimless dark blue felt hat, which would have challenged the ingenuity of a beauty queen.

My contemporaries had pondered the matter and decided that the only acceptable solution was to turn their hat brims up all the way round. But my mother for some reason decided that she preferred my hat brim turned down all the way round. As any thinking adult knows to his cost, the biggest crime one can commit at school is to look or behave in a different way. Being biddable, green and unimaginative, it never occurred to me to argue with my mother and once I turned the corner of the road to turn the wretched brim up so I could slide into school as anonymously as possible, I knew from the beginning I was the subject of derision and to make matters worse my mother had insisted on me carrying an umbrella. I may say that my mother was the least self-conscious person I have ever met and she frequently rode her bicycle with her umbrella up. But these two unacceptable fashion quirks marked me down and the result was that I was bullied unmercifully. Having no conception of how to protect myself, I continued to be utterly miserable and was regularly sick every morning before I set off to meet my tormentors.

Of course life did improve and became manageable, but I have to admit I was never happy at school. My life would have been much easier and more fulfilling if I'd been good at games. My father had an excellent eye for a ball, although he was rather bored with tennis, cricket and golf, preferring to hunt or fish or shoot. He was very capable and succeeded in everything he attempted. My mother was an extremely good games player and, while she was at school, a famous tennis coach had asked grandpa if he could train her with a view to Wimbledon. So with all these genes in my system it seems rather unfair that I had not inherited any of these gifts. I could not even see a ball let alone hit it.

Our games lessons at the High School were taken by students from the Bedford Physical Training College and to me they were some of the most frightening women I have ever met. How strange that one can recall after nearly seventy years the horror of the wall bars from which one was supposed to hang upside down, the horse one was ordered to vault, and the ropes that I never managed to climb. I'm sure our instructors, Brünnhildes all, were models of female fitness and strength, but I thought they were unfeminine and insensitive. My lack of prowess in the gym was even worse on the games field although I must have made some attempt at netball, for I broke a bone in my foot during one game. But help was at hand when Jeff and I moved to the country. From there, I used to bicycle for six miles into Bedford everyday and the daily twelve mile ride allowed me to be exempt from playing games. Battling with a head wind and sometimes driving rain, I knew it was worth it.

Jeff and I were still living in Bedford when war was declared. I remember quite clearly sitting in the kitchen, listening to Mr. Chamberlain's voice breaking the news that would change the world and countless lives forever. It was very frightening and something I could not comprehend.

On that day I was still basking in the excitement and glory of my beloved Vulcan winning the obedience test at Sandy Show three days earlier. Sandy Show was a fairly big agricultural show in these parts and despite the constant loud speaker announcements asking people to take in evacuees from London, the excited crowds were determined to enjoy this occasion, for who knew when it would take place again.

The obedience test for gun dogs was a serious event, which attracted breeders from far and wide. One competitor who took the test extremely seriously was Auntie Mabel. In fact, Auntie Mabel was no relation but she had known my father as a small boy and she shared his passion for yellow Labradors over the years. She became a close friend and loving aunt. She had bred and trained her much loved Ginny, which won a large silver cup for her. So passionate was her interest in dogs and Labradors in particular that one day when she was describing a mutual friend she remarked, 'Oh of course, she was by so and so out of so and so!' Auntie Mabel had been coaching her own dog for weeks and knowing Vulcan and I were to compete against her and various other competitors who wore white kennel coats, I felt rather intimidated, but I need not have worried.

Vulcan was an old dog now but he had been one of D's best-trained Labradors. In his youth, he had followed D at heel right across London, only having to be lifted on and off the moving staircase on the tube. He had sat patiently waiting for D outside a house while a thunderstorm broke out over his head. He was a perfect gentleman and he never let me down. Walking to heel, jumping a hurdle fence to retrieve a dummy, retrieving his dummy out of the river, he was faultless. When the judge handed me the red card he remarked, 'He was a little slow but he did everything you asked him.' I believe the crowds were delighted. One gawky eleven year old and an elderly dog competing against so many professionals made it a popular win, a win to make people laugh and forget for a few minutes, the horrors, the anxieties and the troubles to come. My parents told me afterwards that Auntie Mabel had taken three pages to tell them why she had not won and half a page to describe my win.

What do I remember about these times? Naturally, the sticking tape across the windows, the black-out curtains and the gas masks in their small cardboard boxes which went everywhere with us. We also had identity discs, which we always wore around our necks and Auntie Syb had sent me a little silver St. Anthony and St Christopher to wear too. I have lost these treasures over the years, which is sad, because my little silver saints were very precious to me at that time.

We were not obliged to take in evacuee children when war was declared because our small house became a refuge for D's two aunts, Alice Carrol (we called her Alal) his mother's sister and Sibyl Martyn, his father's sister. Auntie Syb was a complete contrast to Alal. She was small and round and she bubbled with laughter and good temper. Alal was 6 foot 2 and quiet and reserved. Poor darling, we did not realise she was dying of cancer when she moved out of her drab London hotel to come to us. I think that they had very little in common, apart from their deep love for my parents. Auntie Syb was a kind of double aunt, for as well as being Grandpa Scott's sister she had married a brother of Granny James, my mother's mother. Auntie Syb was a devout Roman Catholic and Alal was a fairly conservative member of the Church of Ireland. But there may have been a slight tension between the two because Grandpa Scott had found other loves and interests and left Daddy's mother just before I was born. It was tragic and, on these occasions, families usually take sides.

There were few bombs at that stage of the war and Auntie Syb, homesick for her Chelsea home, returned to London. Jeff was wonderfully thoughtful and very caring to Alal and nursed the old lady as tenderly as her own mother and I'm thankful that Alal did know some love and care at the end and did not die alone in her pain in her London hotel. Her sister Maud had died on the 12 September 1939 just after war was declared and Alal followed her four months later.

The day of Alal's funeral, Jeff sent me out to spend the day with a school friend while she went to the funeral and gave tea to the very few mourners. She had lit a little fire in the dining room and when she went to the front door to let me in, in the evening, she was horrified to see that the dining room chimney was ablaze. She called the fire brigade and Vulcan and I must have let ourselves into the garden. The dining room contained the valuable portrait of my great-great-grandfather Sir William Parker Carrol and the elegant hunting table which D used as a dining room table. To this day we will never know how Jeff and a neighbour managed to manoeuvre it out of the room into the garden because it took four removal men from Pickfords to put it back.

Jeff's next act of courage and devotion came when my parents wrote from India to ask her if she would be willing to take me out to Canada, for a great many children were being sent to Canada to avoid the war at that time. There was no problem about Vulcan, for he had had to be put to sleep a little while before. She bought thick clothes for the cold winters in Nova Scotia, packed up the house and moved us into a hotel where we awaited our sailing orders. I firmly believe that my guardian angel works overtime. We were prevented from sailing because Jeff had put herself down, quite correctly, as my legal guardian rather than my governess and her exit permit was held up. We then heard the devastating news that that ship had been torpedoed. I cannot remember the name of that ship but I certainly remember the name of the next ship in which we would have sailed if my parents had not cabled from India:

CANCEL ALL PLANS FOR GOING TO CANADA.

The name was *The City of Benares*. She was torpedoed by a U-boat in mid-Atlantic with 105 child evacuees on board, 306 of the passengers died, including eighty-five children. The torpedo struck at 10pm on 17 September. It was a night of raging storms and those who survived were rescued by HMS *Hurricane,* spent twenty hours in a lifeboat, or managed to cling to an upturned lifeboat. It was an appalling tragedy. When I saw the headlines in the paper, I went down with my first migraine.

It is now so long ago that I cannot remember if it was before or after this happening that Jeff took in a Jewish Hungarian couple with their little girl of two and a half. Stephen Anders was an agricultural chemist and he and his wife spoke little English but Pannie became the family interpreter. She was a lovely child with dark curly hair and I remember the evening when they invited Jeff and myself into the kitchen to see the table they had laid for one of their Jewish festivals.

I have already confessed that the High School was not my favourite place, but to be honest, being an only child and unused to mixing with other children, I probably would have not been happy at any school. Looking back, I have a vision of a place, which was a cross between a female prison and Jane Eyre's institution; for one thing the classrooms did not show a sign of light or colour. There were no pictures on the walls and shame on them, there was not a map in the place. Our teachers were formidable, blue stockings all, and they must have considered any sign of vanity unnecessary and frivolous, for they thought the sole aim of any young women in those days should be to take up nursing, teaching or missionary work. Dressed in masculine coats and skirts, their hair scraped back into a severe bun or plaited round their heads or shingled, they strode into class making little humming noises, their amber beads bouncing on their ample bosoms.

But of course, there were members of staff of whom I was very fond. Miss Burnaby was gentle and pretty and taught the youngest children. She was always kind and she smiled. Miss Lomax always wore beautifully cut coats and skirts when she took us for history, my favourite lesson. I cannot remember the name of the geography mistress, which is probably just as well. She was a rather a pathetic creature who suffered from halitosis so we used to take turns as to who would have to suffer in the front row. Our geography books did contain small maps, but the only lessons I can remember were based on coal, wood and fish. None of these subjects would seem very useful today and it certainly gave no one the desire to explore the beauties and wonders of our miraculous world.

CHAPTER THREE

Growing Up in Wartime

It seems to be a tradition that most Scripture teachers suffer from a certain amount of ragging unless they're inspired by the old prophets to threaten their class with threats of fire and brimstone. This was not Miss Rayley's way. She was short and slight and gentle and her white hair was dressed in an immaculate Eton crop. I think we were really quite fond of her; however, we were also wicked enough to distract her from her theme with a shoal of red herrings. I well remember her asking, 'Now girls can you tell me what all the apostles had in common?' We gazed piously at the ceiling and suggested the obvious. They were all good and they loved God. 'No girls, they were all men, men with a capital M.' I've always agreed with her reasoning but I was astounded at her knowledge of men with a capital M.

Miss Wilson taught us English and she was perhaps the plainest member of staff but certainly one of the most loveable. I recall her saying it is sad to lose someone you love but it sadder still never to have loved.

I look back upon those wartime years through a child's eyes. Apart from the air raid sirens, the barrage balloons, and the constant queuing for something extra to eat despite our ration books, I recall that every other person appeared to be wearing some kind of uniform.

Jeff was an excellent plain cook and when she gave me my first cooking lessons, they were far more practical than the ones we had at school, where it could take all morning to clean the silver tea pot.

But Bedford was spared the worst of the bombing and I believe we only had two land mines, which were dropped by a German bomber reluctant to take them home. We could see the orange glow of fires in the direction of London and we heard the ominous drone of bombers passing overhead to destroy poor suffering Coventry, but we were undoubtedly lucky. It was for that reason that the BBC Symphony Orchestra was evacuated down to Bedford. We had all the pleasure of listening to a top class orchestra at a time when there was no T.V. and the wireless generally concentrated on Workers' Playtime or music from one of the dance bands. Sir Malcolm Sergeant gave some unforgettable children's concerts, while pianists such as Myra Hess and Solomon gave frequent recitals at the Corn Exchange. Every seat was always taken and we could see through the open door into the alleyway, which was filled with servicemen and women hungry for beauty, for normality and for hope.

Of course, sometimes I saw the true reality of grief and I remember meeting the fiancée of my best friend's older brother, stumbling away from his grave in the cemetery in floods of tears. David Whitley had been young, handsome, and brave and had been lost flying a bomber over Germany. It was heartbreaking, but we were generally sheltered from the worst news of those appalling losses at sea, on land and in the air. So many quietly gave up their lives so that their families and their country could have a future and hopefully the world would become a better place. Our knowledge has grown beyond all expectations in this last century but human nature remains very much the same and we still have a lot to learn in wisdom, tolerance, compassion and common sense.

I cannot remember which year Jeff moved us out to the country. The lease of the semi-detached house in Bedford had run out and she was lucky to be able to rent a bungalow in Pavenhan just over the wall from Auntie Mabel's garden. It was clinker built in wood, attached to a small barn, which may well have been used to store the osiers from the river in past years, but was now a charming room. Apart from being convenient, it had a really lovely view of fields leading down to the River Ouse. Soon after we moved in it came up for sale and my father paused in the middle of a battle in the Arakan to buy it for £1,000.

The year we moved to the country is a watershed in my life for things were never quite the same again. Jeff had been wonderful in caring for me and poor Alal at the beginning of the war, but now a new element came into her life and she fell in love with Rogue, a married chicken farmer. She went to work for him on his small farm as a war job and although we were never short of eggs after that, the affair became secretive, underhand and to me rather shameful. My conscience told me it was all wrong and I was haunted by dread and guilt as if the affair was mine not hers. Once when I heard his car drive away in the early hours of the morning I wished passionately for something horrible to happen to him. My evil thoughts returned to haunt me, for on reaching home he had a seizure and his wife had to telephone Jeff to help her get him out of the car. I was left alone in the bungalow and when I heard footsteps walking round the house and tapping on a window, I was terrified, not realising it was Rogue's son looking for Jeff. Since then I have always been frightened of wishing another person ill. It really doesn't pay. It is far better to leave the problem for God to sort out.

The affair affected my health and my schoolwork. I was growing and developing and I frequently fainted for no apparent reason. But my schoolwork was not only overshadowed by Jeff's love affair. She persuaded the doctor that I was run down and I would be better if I was kept at home from school for a term. This gap in my education was not helped by the fact that she gave me no backup with my homework and I was often cleaning the house when I should have been writing an essay. When I first started school I was nearly always top of my class but now my marks deteriorated and it never occurred to anyone to wonder why. Jeff undoubtedly loved me. I was the child she never had but she was terrified of losing me and probably without realising it she put me off trying for a place at University. Jimmy and I saw similar examples when we were teaching, where a possessive mother would not allow her child to take up a scholarship for a private school in case he outgrew her and was ashamed of his roots. Selfless love is a very rare thing and when an element of possessiveness takes over it can have all kinds of unfortunate consequences.

At the age of fourteen and fifteen I was craving for knowledge and I would lie on the grass at the chicken farm and devour all the classics I could get hold of; Tolstoy, Chekov, Jane Austin, Shakespeare, Victor Hugo. Some of these stories frightened me and there was no one to tell me what to read next but it was all experience. In these permissive times, when anything goes, my attitude to Jeff's sad little affair must seem very narrow, judgmental, and prudish, but I had been brought up by granny to think such behaviour was sinful and the guilt of it all made me ill and unhappy.

1943. Wartime Harvesting.

Although my schoolwork deteriorated, my knowledge of farming and the countryside grew. I learned to milk cows and make butter; I cleaned out cowsheds and even took the bull to the cow although I was sent home before any action took place. I learned to rub salt and brown sugar into sides of bacon, to put eggs into waterglass, make jam and cook porridge in a hay box. I hoed onions and planted potatoes and when the harvest came there was plenty to do stooking the corn and helping with the threshing afterwards. It was another side of life and I loved it but I could never enjoy helping with the poor wretched battery hens in their cramped little wire cages. Sometimes they lost their reason and ate their own feathers and the feathers of their companions and who could blame the poor things. Hens are not the most intelligent of creatures, but there is a vast difference between the restless, agitated, staring-eyed birds kept in batteries and the placid, contented birds, which are allowed their freedom to move and enjoy their surroundings.

When the summer holidays came, I spent a great part of them in Gloucestershire with a dear friend of my father's mother. Lady Kathleen Lindsay was a widow and she lived with her daughter and son-in-law, Doreen and Dick Archer Houblon. Auntie Kathleen worked in a munitions factory throughout the war and Doreen did a variety of war jobs including running a harvest camp for boys from St. Paul's School. I was brought in to help cook as well as helping in the harvest fields. This was another break with granny's teaching. How could one avoid boys when one was thrust amongst so many? Fortunately they were as disinterested in me as I was nervous of them, although my morale was boosted when one young man said I look like Glynis Johns in *49th Parallel*. I had not seen the film but it sounded encouraging.

Dick Archer Houblon lived the life of a semi-invalid because he had been gassed in the First World War, but I grew to be very fond of him. He was gentle and kind and taught me about birds. Doreen and her mother were also very kind but not demonstrative in their affection and I never knew if I would return to a empty house or a bridge party in full spate when I returned from the harvest field. I was also demoralised when I overheard Doreen remark to her mother, 'She's just like her mother, a bundle of nerves!' It was probably true but my confidence received another dent. Doreen was a beautiful horsewoman and an expert on side-saddle in her day. In later years, she frequently stood in for the Queen at the rehearsal for the trooping of the colour. My biggest treat was to go out riding before breakfast with Auntie Kathleen. The sky would still be flushed with the pink of dawn and the dew heavy on the grass when we rode out from the stables. The beauty and the peace of those early morning rides were unforgettable and war seemed far away.

Auntie Mabel was highly suspicious of the goings on over her garden wall and wrote to India to tell my parents. My father was fighting in Burma and my mother was beginning to plan her return home, as losses at sea and the danger of sinking in the convoys were growing less. My father had forbidden her to return sooner in case I ended up with no parents at all. My mother wrote to Jeff and taxed her with Auntie Mabel's comments. Jeff denied everything but fear, guilt and insecurity caused her to mount a secret propaganda war to make me believe my mother was a nymphomaniac and a drug addict. I refused to accept this but it was a difficult time because Jeff had cared for me with great devotion for many years and I found it hard to hate her. My parents gave her a substantial cheque in gratitude for all she had done and Jeff found another job in Bedfordshire. But she informed the family she had been sacked after years of devoted service. This was quite untrue and how could she expect my parents to employ her when they were there to take over.

One day Jeff came to meet me on my school bus to continue her subversive brainwashing. I think she realised then, by my cool reception that she could not win, for we never met again. But there are always some in the family who for reasons of their own jealousy and envy are delighted to except such damaging tales as gospel truth and my mother's youngest sister Trill and my father's cousin Rosaleen delighted in hearing stories against my poor mother and refused to listen to the other side of the question. My mother was a darling, generous, loving and kind and she worshipped my father. It was sad that she had to suffer from this shadow over relationships.

Time healed, but it was unjust and an unhappy end to a friendship, which had been founded on trust and affection. I was thrilled to be with my parents again and although I had been a child when they last saw me, I was now seventeen and it was as if we had never been apart. My father became my hero, he had always been my mother's, and in my relief and happiness, I agreed to all their suggestions. I was taken up to Elizabeth Arden in Bond Street to be taught how to put on my makeup and my mother had me fitted, as she had been all her life, with lace-up corsets. I endured these whalebone instruments of torture until I was well into my twenties when we went to live in Singapore, when for some reason my mother had pity on me. She continued to wear her own stays until she was nearly eighty.

Then came the great question as to what I should do with my life. In those years just after the war, I suppose most parents regarded marriage as the perfect solution, but my father certainly couldn't afford to bring me out in the London season and, after being caught up with jobs in the war, most girls refused to sit and wait to be proposed to but took on various careers which would have not been contemplated before. I had no strong feelings on the subject although I vaguely contemplated being a dietician at one stage. I had managed to pass my school certificate by the narrowest of margins but I had little to offer. Then my mother remembered her friendship with Norman Hartnell's sister. My parents thought over the problem and decided that if I entered the world of haute couture, in time, I could work my way up to becoming a buyer and buyers not only made money, something the family was always short of, but had opportunities to travel and meet people. They overlooked one or two important factors. The first one was that although I enjoyed having a pretty dress, I was not especially interested in clothes, and the second was that money sense was not one of my attributes. Nevertheless, if my parents thought it was right, it must be.

CHAPTER FOUR

Haute Couture

~~~~~~~~~~~~~~~~~~~~~~~~~~~~~~~~~~~~

My home during the week was in a residential club for educated working ladies. In other words, it was a hostel. I can not recall how many there were of us tucked into the minute cell-like rooms of St. Clement's, but my room was on the top floor and was unique in having two doors and two numbers, 154 and 153. I think even St. Clement's had considered that 153 on its own would be uncomfortable for a midget and so they joined it onto 154. This was a tremendous bonus because we were only allowed a bath on alternative nights, depending whether ones room had an odd or even number and I had no hesitation in asking the current occupant of the bathroom to knock on 153 on odd nights and 154 on even. There was just room for a bed, a small cupboard, a chair, a bookcase, and a dressing table. But I was terribly proud of it; for my mother had given me pretty cushions for my bed, and we even found some export reject cups and saucers, with flowers on them rather than the usual utility white.

I made some good friends at St. Clement's for there were some delightful girls there. Most of them appeared to be involved in medicine in one form or another and when the conversation at the supper table became very technical I pleaded for a respite until we had finished our prunes and custard. I suppose most of us were in our late teens and early twenties, except for two middle-aged lesbians who had adjoining rooms on the top floor. They only talked to each other and I was intrigued to discover one boiling down her lipstick ends on one of the gas rings we used to heat the kettles and saucepans.

I started work in one of Norman Hartnell's workrooms in the winter of 1946. I well remember my first glimpse of the workroom. After taking out my card and having it punched, I was shown into a long room on the ground floor, looking over a mews. The scene that met my eyes was really Dickensian. There were power cuts at that period and the only light came from rows of candles, which stood in the centre of the long worktables. The tables were covered with white sheets and in the evenings these were folded over our sewing to keep it clean for the morning. Every workroom had a fitter (archangel status), two cutters and perhaps a dozen hands, girls who were in sole charge of making up a dress. Each hand had one assistant and if she was lucky, an apprentice who was the lowest form of life. I started as an apprentice and I was given one pound eleven shillings and two pence a week.

I had been apprehensive about my reception because these girls had been working since they were fourteen and their backgrounds were unlike my own, but I was lucky. They were incredibly kind to me. Although the work was taxing, we were able to gossip across the table. Emily was the head hand in our workroom, she must have been well into her sixties, and she sat opposite Doris who had a clubfoot and unfortunate teeth. Eveline was my hand and although she was probably only a few months older than me, she was a very hard task-master. I had worked on buttonholing for three weeks before I was promoted to over-sewing and making pads. At that time the woollen fabric needed to make up a dress had to be shrunk. We were not allowed to have electric irons because years before a girl had dropped one and broken it. Instead, a row of flat irons stood heating over gas jets. Shrinking material was a miserable occupation because one had to press the material all over with a damp cloth and a red-hot flat iron. The steam rose in scalding clouds making one's hands red and sore. Eveline was a beautiful needlewoman, but no sergeant major could have been fiercer in her criticism of slapdash work and I have returned to my room in St. Clement's in tears because of some clumsy stitching on Lady B's sleeves.

One day I was working on the inside of a stage dress for Elsie Waters. Elsie and Doris were good friends of my parents, for when they toured the Far East to entertain the troops during the war, my father or D as I always called him called two of his guns Elsie and Doris after them. Their stage dresses were always identical and I remember this one was made of soft coral coloured crepe. Obviously, I was not thinking what I was doing, for I noticed a lot of untidy loose ends on the inside of the dress, which appeared to have no place there and so I cut them off. Even after all these years I can still hear the faint smack as a bunch of sequin roses fell under the workroom table. It must have taken the embroideress about two weeks to complete. Surprisingly, I did not receive my cards.

I was always surprised that the girls who sewed these beautiful creations were not resentful of the spoiled beauties that wore them. I suppose they felt they were all part of the glamour in that world of fantastic dreams, but after a trying day I sometimes felt like erecting a guillotine in Berkley Square. Eveline was strict but occasionally I could distract her by asking her about her boyfriend, Bill. Then her eyes became soft and misty and we could look forward to a quiet morning. Bill's job in life was to stick up large posters on the hoardings in the underground. I often had a macabre picture of poor Bill complete with glue pot and ladder scampering out of a tunnel when the first train of the morning arrived.

The workroom girls had two passions. Half of them followed the speedway riders and the other half were devoted to opera. This may have been encouraged, because one girl with a very sweet voice dreamed of the day when she might be accepted for the chorus of Covent Garden. I never went to a speedway meeting; those riders were lucky because sometimes they would receive exotic silk ties made by their fans, from the cuttings on the workroom floor. But those who loved music took me to see my very first opera *Il Trovatore*. I loved it until I tried to retell D the story.

One of the party was Dolores, Hartnell's chief model. She was very beautiful with her long dark hair and olive skin and a figure as graceful and as lissom as a Siamese cat. Before a show, some of the apprentices were sent up to the model room to help dress the models for their quick changes. I always tried to dress Dolores and we became good friends, which lasted until her death a few years ago. Under her glamorous, sophisticated image, she was very sincere and infinitely kind. She filled in her waiting moments painting and collecting stamps and at the end of the day she creamed off her makeup and returned home to care for her elderly father and her dog. It was Dolores who taught me how to walk in the four inch heeled shoes, which she gave me. Unfortunately, I chose to show off when D took me to the Chelsea Flower show and as he liked to start off with manure and end up with orchids, I walked back to St. Clement's in my stocking feet.

I was sewing in the workroom at the time of Princess Elizabeth's wedding to Prince Philip and, as our room led on to the mews, we were occasionally invaded by the press, who tried to photograph every dustsheet in sight. We were all taken up to the showroom the day before the wedding to see the wedding dress displayed on a stand. It was really beautiful, so simple with very dainty embroidery and after the utility fashions of the war years; it was a breath of spring and hope to come. In our workroom, we made the Queen Mother's gold lamé dress and Queen Mary's dress of soft blue velvet and gold. We were all allowed to have snippets of material from these historic creations and I still have mine, which include a piece of the wedding dress about the size of a postage stamp.

The first batch of material for the hydrangea blue going away dress was taken from the stockroom and I never heard the end of that drama. Miss Yvonne, the Queen's vendeuse, told us that behind the scenes at the palace it was just like any family wedding. The king was glad to have a small drink before he set out with the princess. She refused any drink and was completely calm and radiantly happy. It was poor Miss Yvonne who found herself in trouble. Tucking the train of the dress into the carriage she caught the heel of her own dress and fell face down into the carriage almost on top of the princess. The king was most concerned, picked her up, and dusted her down and everybody set off in good time. I'm glad Miss Yvonne had her own little adventure. She was a very sweet woman and shortly afterwards she died from cancer.

In the workroom, we made our own fun and when there was a staff dance – it was in the days of the Lambeth Walk and the Hokey Cokey – I took D as my partner. He was a tremendous success and he danced and flirted with all the girls, who thought he was gorgeous. We once had an impromptu dance in the mews, which could be a very smelly place in high summer. At about the time we stopped for our lunch break, an upright piano was wheeled outside our door and its owner began to play. It was like a scene from *Salad Days*, we girls danced in the street totally unselfconscious and filled with the gaiety of the music. I cannot think the pianist received many pennies, because we did not possess them, but he gave me a memory of spontaneous happiness that has remained with me over the years.

I spent two years with my friends in the workroom and although they taught me to sew I could have never have achieved their standard and I sometimes wondered rather bleakly what I was doing there and where it was leading. But at the end of the war, I think few daughters would have wished to go against their parent's wishes, especially when they had been taking so much trouble to see them settled. But I did make one change; I asked if I could go into the showroom. I became an assistant to a very sweet vendeuse named Miss Kelsey. She was stately and very kind and she had a purple rinse rather like Madame Jean who was head of the showroom and always used a pencil to dial her telephone numbers. We all wore soft, lichen-green dresses. Norman Hartnell had created the colour himself and the carpet and all the furnishings in the showroom were the same colour, so you could have been working in a mysterious fairy tale world at the bottom of the sea.

The competition between the vendeuses was intense, because they were nearly all to some extent on commission and they watched each other's customers with the intensity of a terrier at a rat hole. The showroom had its various departments and each one had its own dictator who was confident that without her expertise the whole fashion house would collapse. This included Louise in the stockroom who gave out the material and Florrie in the packing room who lived in a world of gold embossed boxes and tissue paper and dispatched the various finished garments to their future homes. Miss Godley, the business manageress had her kingdom, which was only reached by an iron spiral staircase. *Debrett* and *Who's Who* were her bibles and every now and again she would descend from her eyrie and tell us on no account to accept an order from Lady X. because she would never be able to pay. In contrast to this we had one customer from South Africa whose dress allowance came from her husband's diamonds. She generally ordered about five dresses and she would sit on the green staircase leading to the upper rooms with her skirt tucked up and her legs rather unbecomingly apart and solemnly count out the bank notes one by one into her vendeuse's thankful hands.

We had a minor crisis one day, when Lynda Christian arrived with her husband. Tyrone Power, to have a fitting for the five dresses she had ordered. As she was expecting a baby in the not too distant future, this was a very tricky situation for her fitter. Should she let the dress out two or three inches for the next fitting? But that particular day the problem was hunger. Although she had lunched at the Savoy, Lynda said she was starving and she simply must have something to eat. The canteen had closed and nobody on the premises had anything eatable until it was discovered that Miss Godley had one solitary current bun, which she had been saving for her own tea.

I met some interesting clients while I was in the showroom, some famous, some notorious, some very, very trying. The comediennes like Elsie and Doris were always delightful to everyone and I once summoned up all my courage and asked Beryl Grey to tell me about her most exciting moment when she was performing at Covent Garden. Her eyes lit up and she replied, 'Oh at the end of the ballet, when we'd come out in front of the huge red curtain and I'd see all the people sitting all around the opera house.' She was a lovely person, completely natural and kind. The straight actresses were the most difficult, like those with newly acquired wealth. They were super fussy and frequently rude, for they were completely self absorbed and seldom had any sense of humour. Miss Kelsey would not allow me into the fitting room when one celebrated star of the West End stage had a fitting, because she never wore any knickers.

Very occasionally, Miss Kelsey would give one of her clients to me. There was one tragic elderly woman who lived in lonely splendour in St. Johns Wood. She was really a gentle little soul but she can't have had many friends, for at least three times a week she shopped in Bond Street and then came on to view the collection, which she must have known by heart. Miss Kelsey was patient, but you can have enough of a good thing and so I accepted the challenge and took Mrs. G. to a fitting room to try on a charming flowered silk dress, which had a skirt in layers like an unopened tulip bud. Mrs. G. was a little birdlike creature and to this day I shall never know how it happened but she slipped the dress over her head and shoulders and than stuck. Round and round the fitting room we waltzed with Mrs. G. looking like the rear end of a pantomime horse. Somehow I managed to get her out of it but then she developed a nosebleed and none of the fitting rooms had a key. In a strange way, I think the small adventure enlivened her usual routine, because she never blamed me, but after that, she only came in to see the collection twice a week.

Florrie, in the packing room was a delightful Cockney and usually very helpful. But on the one day that Miss Kelsey was away with a cold and I was in sole charge of all her clients, Florrie decided that she was getting a cold too and was not going to be hassled or bothered. 'But Florrie, you know Lady S. is a very good customer and she wants to wear her dress at a reception tonight.' 'Tell the old cow to wait, I'm sick of all this 'hautie' couture', replied Florrie reaching for the Kleenex. This was horrendous news, no dress, no reception, and no client. I went to the telephone and dialled Lady S's number. 'Forgive me for worrying you madam, but our delivery van has broken down. I will bring your dress round in a taxi.' I was collecting my coat when I discovered that Florrie had relented and dispatched the dress on its way. Once again, I approached the telephone. 'I thought I'd let you know Madam, our delivery van is bringing your dress on its way to the garage.'

Today, most British workmen will wolf whistle at any pretty girl, but in the late forties, they must have been made of sterner stuff. We were not faced then with everything from cars to telephones being labelled sexy. One grey afternoon I was alone on duty in the showroom while Barbara Goalen was being photographed in one of

1948. Norman Hartnell's showroom.

Hartnell's most breathtakingly beautiful evening gown. The wide skirt and bodice and long sleeves were encrusted with turquoise sequins, the final touch being a soft shocking pink velvet collar. Barbara Goalen was a legendary beauty of her time and as she half lay, half reclined on the cushions on the showroom floor, the effect was stunning. But at that moment the window opened. 26 Bruton Street was being painted on the outside and in through the window came two painters, one long ladder, and two tins of dangerously dripping paint. They didn't appear to glance at Barbara but they managed to step over her and she just avoided a crack on the head with the end of the ladder. 'Come on Bert', said the leading painter. 'If we get a move on, we'll find out what won the three thirty.'

I was rather shocked to discover that those in the showroom usually regarded the girls in the workroom as less than dirt, at any rate not worth their attention. This was not only unjust and unkind but also very silly, because they would have certainly received no commission without them. When I went into the showroom I tried in a small way to remedy this by telling the hands concerned with the making up of a dress how thrilled a lady was with her dress; 'Lady Y had said that everybody had admired it, including the Duchess of X.' They would drink this in and be really delighted, so if Lady Y had not said a word I would occasionally make it up. I think we all like to be appreciated, to be thanked, and to feel our labours are being valued.

I was fortunate to work for Hartnell's at the time I did. The war was over and women were able to discard some of the plain utility dresses, save up their dress coupons and celebrate in some of the utterly feminine, devastatingly pretty dresses which had the 'New Look'. Norman Hartnell must have designed about fifty dresses for a season, I'm guessing here, and he had a special talent for creating embroidered evening gowns.

The fitter would take his sketches to her workroom and drape and pin, and pleat and cut out the first model with the help of the cutter. These exclusive gowns were shown to his clients by four or five models and the quick changes behind the scenes had to be like lightning. Then Lady Y or Mrs C would decide that she wanted to order Winter Rose or Ascot Day for herself. Her vendeuse would summon the fitter with her tape measure and then it was all down to the workroom to create Mrs Y's own dress. Miss Kelsey asked me once if I would like to become a model but I refused. My measurements would have given no problem but I knew I was basically too shy and nervous to be able to put on a happy, carefree 'aren't I pretty' look.

It was glamorous and exciting, but I would walk home to St Clement's in the evening with a feeling of depression, which not even Dick Barton could lift. What on earth good was I doing with my life, what had I achieved? That day I had managed to boost the morale of an agitated mother of a bride and I knew she was going to look delightful for her daughter's wedding. But it all seemed rather superficial and how on earth was I to tell my parents this was not the life for me? My problem was solved when my father was made a Major General commanding Hamburg Base District and he wanted me to go to Germany with him and my mother. But I'm overlooking the most important part of my life; Jimmy.

CHAPTER FIVE

Enter Jimmy

Jimmy's uncle had been D's best man and my godfather, and we had first met when the Scott family was invited to stay with the Robertsons for Easter 1929. Molly Robertson, Jimmy's mother was sister to Col. Jack Wills my godfather. I suppose the friendship between Nunky as I learned to call Uncle Jack and D really started when D arrived at Aldershot as a carefree, unattached subaltern. He was followed by what might have appeared to be a private circus. Two horses, a terrier bitch with a litter of puppies, a couple of ferrets, and some fishing rods. I don't think D had any hawks at that time, but it was enough to catch Nunky's attention and thinking D might be worth knowing, he offered him a camp bed in his room, as all the other rooms were taken. It was the beginning of a lifetime friendship.

The arrival of the Scotts at Easter must have been almost as dramatic. My parents, my nanny and I were all squeezed into the baby Austin with two Labradors and, as my mother always prepared for any emergency; I imagine our luggage was tied on all over the car. Jimmy was eight, staying at home to recover from pneumonia and I was eleven months old. He was in disgrace having stolen my rusks. It was his sister who suggested this felony and I think he must have been rather bored with that baby. However his mother said, 'Say goodnight to June', as my nanny carried me up to bed and he came up to me and kissed me. My mother turned to Jimmy's mother in astonishment. 'Molly dear, right on the mouth!'

We met again very briefly when I was five, and I was aware he existed during the war when Nunky remarked to me, 'I'm very proud of my nephew, he's just recovered from polio and now he's doing a parachuting course.' I remember thinking, what a hero, I shall never meet anyone like that, but we met properly when I was seventeen and he was twenty-five. Auntie Mabel had told my parents that she had been saving up her petrol coupons and wouldn't it be fun if we drove over to Berkhamstad to see the Robertsons. We had Labradors in common. We arrived and were taken down to the field to see Jimmy's horse. He himself arrived home in uniform for a weekend leave a few minutes later and I thought I'd never seen a more wonderful being. He was tall; six foot three, with broad shoulders and beautiful clear grey eyes under straight brows. He had a firm chin and a sensitive mouth. His smile was stunning; starting in his eyes and he had a most attractive speaking voice. Faced with this God-like creature, I said an inward prayer. Dear God let him love me. My guardian angel nodded in approval and answered my prayer but I'd not thought it

Easter 1929. Jimmy aged 8 with his parents, sister and my nanny holding me – our first meeting!

out. I loved him but it was too soon and out of my confused girl-hood, D was the man in my life who I turned to with any problem. I felt this was not the right basis for marriage because following in my grandmother's and mother's footsteps, marriage was something never taken lightly and when you married, your husband and his interests should always come first. Also I was shy, green, and rather prudish and I'd not learned to laugh at myself.

Jimmy was protective, gentle, and almost reverential in his wooing and in after years we used to laugh and wonder what my reaction would have been, if he'd shaken me. As it was, he proposed to me at intervals over the next four years. Jimmy was the least vain man I've ever met. J.F. Roxburgh, his headmaster at Stowe, once wrote on his school report: *if he brushed his hair once this term I did not happen to see him on that day.* He was exemplary in uniform and looked gor-geous, but clothes and especially new clothes were very low down on his list of priorities. I think the only arguments we ever had in forty-two years of married life was when I persuaded, or very occa-sionally ordered him to get some new clothes. When it came to my clothes, he undoubtedly liked me to look well, but his first question was, 'Is it comfortable?' It would never occur to him to buy me any seductive undies and on the one occasion I was persuaded to buy a baby doll nightdress by some girlfriends, he took one look at me and said, 'Good God!' I never wore it.

In those very early days when he first started to take me out in London, he must have had several shocks. D had returned from Burma to find he had the novelty of a grown up daughter and, instead of choosing soft pastel shades for my clothes, he very often decided on black. I claim to have 'come out' at a boxing match at the Albert Hall. It was certainly my first grown up occasion and as it was service boxing, nobody was in the ring long enough to get badly hurt. I remember that evening quite well for in the middle of one of the struggling, panting finals a woman in the front row rose to her feet, with a slight scream and cried out, 'My fish pie!' I think D thought boxing would be a good antidote to too much haute couture.

I was terribly hat conscious at that time. I had borrowed some of my mother's hats and I had little hats with eye veils and Hartnell's models, which I'd acquired at cost price, with feathers through the brim or covering the crown and falling over one side of my face. On one occasion when Jimmy called for me to take me out, I was wearing my newest hat, which had been designed by D. It was a neat tricorn with a pussycat bow of veiling. Jimmy looked slightly stunned, but he smiled sweetly and said, 'I thought we would go to the Zoo.' The first time he ever took me out without his sister to chaperone us, we went to Madam Tussaud's to see the Chamber of Horrors.

Over those four years, he was called upon to serve in Italy and Palestine, but he always returned and proposed to me once again and in the intervals between, if any other man started to become serious I would shamelessly use Jimmy as a perfect excuse and say, 'I'm very sorry, but there's somebody else.' It seemed rather kinder than saying, ' I couldn't bear to marry you.' Poor darling Jimmy, I shall never know why he was so patient and long suffering, but when I told him I was going to Germany he quite rightly held a pistol to my head and said I must decide. Once again I told him I did not love him enough. After that, we had no communication whatsoever for the next seven years. I burnt all his photographs except one and wondered about the future.

There was no time to grieve about my love affair, for life was changing rapidly. I was to live in a new country, in a new house and lead a new life. D had been given command of Hamburg Base District in 1949. This entitled him to an ADC, a gracious house overlooking the River Elbe, a large German domestic staff, his own launch and his own train. Well, it wasn't really a train but it was certainly a large coach, which I believe had been used by Goering. D had had a tough war with the Fourteenth Army and after all those years of stress and endurance it seemed right that he could enjoy a little luxury with his family. Having had to face the Japanese, it was probably a sensible decision to place him in Germany where he would have no bitter memories of battles against the armies of Nazi dictators. He was determined to help with the process of restoring peaceful communications and self-respect to our former enemies.

The older generation of Germans might be difficult to win over, but D organised a ball for the young who had no sad memories to overcome. So his young officers danced with charming girls from ancient German families and everyone relaxed and had a happy evening. He also sacked the batman whom he had taken over with the house, when he discovered he was bullying the German staff. Apart from Verner the chef, there was Angred the parlour maid, Irma the housemaid, mummy's own personal maid Irna, who had a permanently haunted expression and the German driver of the Volkswagen. We also had two military drivers living in the house. The senior driver was a Scotsman and D discovered to his cost that it is unwise to give leave to any Scotsman on the 2 January, when poor Prentice fell down a flight steps into the men's mess room after seeing in the New Year. Ellis, D's batman, was kindly, but gormless and lovesick and D's ADC Tony said to Mummy, 'You know Mrs. Scott, I think Ellis has reached saturation point in rockets.' We also had a sad little German from the eastern zone who used to pluck the game in the boiler room, sitting there murmuring, 'quack quack quack,' and created havoc in the garden. I think the reason we had such a vast staff was it gave occupation to many lost, unhappy, displaced people. My parents treated everyone as part as their family and I believe ours was a happy, contented house.

One of my fondest memories was the evening when we all sang *Silent Night* round a big Christmas tree, which had been decorated by the German staff. My parents entertained extensively and here I was face with a problem. I was so shy and nervous of meeting strangers that my hand tended to shake when I was holding a glass. To my consternation, I discovered that some of our guests were equally nervous of dining at the General's house, so I determined to concentrate very hard on making them feel relaxed and at home. I believe it helped them and it certainly made me forget my own inadequacy.

Our house had belonged to a prosperous German businessman and was extremely comfortable, with triple- glazed windows and central heating, which was a new experience for us all. It had been built on a hill just outside Hamburg and there was a stunning view over the river Elbe from the dining room and drawing room windows. There was a large pair of binoculars in the dining room, which must have come from a naval vessel, so we could have a clear view of all the shipping, which passed, up and down the river. The previous General and his wife had had a frightening experience when an intruder held them up in their bedroom at knifepoint. After that, there was always a German policeman on guard outside in the garden.

My parents had taken two of their Labradors out with them. Ben was yellow and Brent was black but they were litter brothers. They were adorable dogs except for the rare occasions when they attacked each other. They'd inherited this unfortunate tendency from their mother Reeve who loved fighting too and on one occasion attacked another dog on her way to be stitched up by the vet. But one particular evening when my mother and I were alone, we let the dogs out in the garden and then to our horror we found they had attacked the German policeman whose trousers were flapping like a loose jib. We sat him down in the dining room and gave him hot sweet tea for shock and I can still hear my mother saying, 'You must let my daughter mend them for you, she was trained at Norman Hartnell.' Needless to say, the policeman could not speak a word of English but I think he realised how sorry we were and the next day he was presented with a new pair of trousers.

It was a time of general tension, because the war was so newly over and nobody knew what the Russians would do. While we were in Hamburg, we were caught up with the preparations for the airlift to Berlin, but D had been given one piece of equipment, which was only to be used if we saw Russian parachutists landing on the lawn. It was a bright red telephone and it stood in solemn state on the grand piano. My mother and I tended to keep it at a distance. One afternoon my mother was alone in the drawing room and the red telephone rang. She was strong in an emergency and she answered it – with a slightly shaky hand. A woman's voice sounded at the other end. 'Tina darling, will you tell Tony to bring a dinner jacket.' My mother was astounded to recognise another General's wife. 'Nell what on earth are you doing on this telephone?' 'Oh', came the reply, 'I always use it, it's so much quicker.'

One of the great benefits of living in Hamburg was that we could frequently go to the opera. It was an excellent way of entertaining guests and we all loved it. We were all very excited when Tony and I were invited to take part in a production of Terence Rattigan's *The Browning Version* at the Grand Theatre in Hamburg. Tony had quite an important part. He was the young housemaster who was about to replace poor tormented Crocker Harris and I was Tony's wife. I had one line, 'Look darling, they've got a garden!' I was dreadfully disappointed when I saw a film of the play many years afterwards to find they had left out my part completely, but after that I was tested and accepted to play a part in the *Passing of the Third Floor Back,* which was being produced on British Forces Network. I think I would have enjoyed that for nobody could see me, but before it took place D was ordered to Singapore.

D was passionate about all field sports and in Germany he could not only go after wild fowl but also roebuck. He got on admirably with all the German hunters, for as countrymen they all spoke the same language and I still cherish the German hunting knife, which they gave him, but I believe he had the greatest fun wild fowling. There were a number of officers on his staff who shared his enthusiasm as well as several naval officers and this is where his launch really came into its own. Sometimes D's enthusiasm was too ambitious. Having been invited to a party on the other side of the Elbe, he decided to go by launch accompanied by several guests including one of two senior ladies. He did not consult the weather forecast and the whole company had a very rough crossing. D's counterpart Admiral Macintosh very wisely decided to drive round by road. When D was called upon to inspect a vehicle maintenance unit, which employed German mechanics, he quite deliberately put on field boots, breeches and wore his eyeglass before addressing them in German. I think he did much to boost their self-respect and they enjoyed it.

My poor mother was not very well over this time and I often had to deputise for her. She was also going through the miserable experience of having to have several teeth removed. After the operation, the doctors decided to keep her in the hospital overnight and I was told to take her a clean nightdress and anything she might need. The German driver drove me in the Volkswagen and I will never forget that dark eerie drive to the military hospital on the other side of Hamburg. We drove for what seemed many miles, through bomb-shattered buildings, which had been flattened in preparation for rebuilding. The landscape was as grey and strange as the surface of the moon, the only colour being the occasional blue cross, which had been painted on a building, presumably where some bodies still lay among the rubble. It was good for me to see the other side of that great city. I knew that houses and offices could be rebuilt but it would take a little longer to rebuild men's lives and bring hope and self-respect back to a nation.

While I was in Hamburg I was invited to stay with old friends of my parents who were living in Oslo. Ken Tressider was a military attaché in Norway and he and Ena lived in a delightful house in Oslo overlooking the fiord. They had been most thoughtful and kind in thinking out various schemes to entertain me, but one morning at breakfast Ken remarked, 'Well, if you two have nothing planned for this morning I believe there is some sort of band concert on at the castle.' My immediate question was, what shall I wear and Ena replied, 'Oh if in doubt wear a hat and shake hands.'

In due course we arrived at the castle where a large crowd had gathered. There was a Norwegian army band drawn up in full dress uniform with rows of seats. The front seats were painted gold. We were astonished to discover that we seemed to be expected. The crowd parted as we arrived and a most important looking officer conducted us to the golden chairs. Ena was Irish and quite imperturbable and I tried to follow her lead and hold her mackintosh, while she carried off the next hour with the authority and calm of Queen Mary. We sat down while the band played and stood up when it stopped and then Ena was asked to inspect the band and pin decorations on them including a particularly large decoration on the conductor. We looked enthusiastic and gratified and managed to hide the fact that we had not a clue what it was all about. When we were eventually taken into the mess we were given large glasses of sherry and we discovered that during the war a Yorkshire regiment, just as well I can't remember which one, had appropriated a Norwegian military march to play for themselves and after the war was over they decided it would be a friendly gesture to give the Norwegians a march of their own in return. Ena had just decorated the Norwegian composer and the entire band. When we returned to lunch, Ken was relaxing over the paper. 'Did you have a good morning Darling?' Ena purred. 'Yes, there was nothing happening in the office, so I had a round of golf,' replied the military attaché.

Besides entertaining guests for lunch and dinner, we often entertained official guests to stay while we were in Hamburg. Edwina, Countess of Mountbatten, stayed with us when she was inspecting the St. John's Ambulance units in Germany. She was charming and super efficient but very autocratic. When she said goodbye to my parents at the front door, she glanced at Tony, D's ADC, and said' You can come with me.' There was no please; that was that and poor Tony had not had his breakfast.

We also entertained Cuthbert Bardesley, Bishop to the forces, who went on to become Bishop of Coventry. He was a dear with a lovely sense of humour. He entertained us with stories of how he'd been invited to preach at St. Paul's Cathedral and in his rush he'd picked up the wrong case so instead of all his vestments, he was faced with his cricket gear. He also told us how once he had arrived to stay with the parents of his small godson rather late in the evening and had been told that the child had gone to bed. He begged permission to say goodnight to him and, on opening the bedroom door, he saw the little boy, head bent, on his knees on the far side of the bed. Not wishing to disturb his prayers Cuthbert knelt down on his side of the bed and said his own. The child looked up with round eyes and asked, "What are you doing?"

"The same as you," Cuthbert replied.

"Well," said the child, "Mummie will be awfully cross. There isn't one on your side".

We also had the Labour appointed Control Commissioner for Schleswig-Holstein, Will Ashbury and his wife May. Will had worked for the railways all his life and he still looked like a kindly Yorkshire stationmaster. He and May found themselves living in half a beautiful Schloss, the other half being occupied by the German family who owned the vast estate. The Ashburys had no experience of such grandeur and certainly no knowledge of diplomatic protocol, but because they were such lovely people, they were a tremendous success. They had an excellent housekeeper who ran the house and briefed them as much as she could, but Will, and May captured everyone's hearts by being thoroughly natural and never pretending they knew something when they did not. They treated all the foreign dignitaries like May's local Women's Institute in Yorkshire. Members of the Diplomatic Corps and senior service officers, Will and May welcomed all in and encouraged them to take part in Sir Roger de Coverley and guessing games and they all loved it. The Ashbury's welcome was warm and sincere and unstuffy, what better ambassadors for this country.

CHAPTER SIX

A Far From Competent Secretary

We were all very happy in Germany and filled with mixed feelings when we heard D had been given command of Singapore Base District. We had a comfortable voyage out and D was able to take me ashore at Aden, Port Said, Bombay and Penang, which was all very exciting because I had no experience of these romantic sounding places, which sound so thrilling and can be so overpoweringly hot.

Our house in Singapore was an old one, with a wide veranda and shutters and fans in every room and heaters in our wardrobes to stop our shoes and dresses turning green with the moist air. We also had five lightning conductors round the house, which was built on a slight hill and when the sudden tropical storms blew up the lightning would strike the conductors like a whiplash. I had always thought

Draycot House, Official Residence of General Officer Commanding Singapore Base District, circa 1952

that lightning storms were pretty and rather exciting in England but after Singapore, I changed my mind.

For the first few months we spent at Draycot House we were dogged by workmen. The house had recently been bought as a permanent residence for the GOC and there were many urgent repairs to be done. The most pressing need was the roof. When it rained and in that part of the world it did not rain in a gentle considerate fashion, it bucketed down as if a tap had been turned on at full pressure, so we had a permanent array of buckets and dishes in the upstairs drawing room. The kitchen also needed a complete refurbishment if we were not to collapse with tummy upsets. All these tasks were tackled by a patient, smiling army of Chinese women. All day long they toiled in the heat dressed in what appeared to be dark blue smocks with large red coolie hats. They carried their small bundles at the end of long swinging bamboo canes and their philosophy was, carry a little frequently, where my reaction would've been treble the load, but probably exhaust myself carrying it. They spoke no English but always nodded and smiled, even when they walked into D's dressing room one morning to find him with very little on. Undismayed, they calmly removed his dressing room door.

I was woken one morning to see two brown legs dangling through the ceiling above my head. It's not very easy to live in a house with so much upheaval but it eventually passed and we felt very proud of ourselves. We had to call out Sammy the Indian foreman on one occasion, which had nothing to do with repairs. We'd had a fairly heavy-going dinner party with the Governor and the Senior Doctor and his wife and many other guests. D was an excellent host, but we did have to work that evening. After dinner my mother led the ladies upstairs to her bedroom and we suddenly realised the Senior Doctor's wife had not reappeared from the loo. When she finally emerged, she looked white and rather shaken, and was obviously very upset. 'I dropped my wedding ring down the pan,' she gasped. The other women were naturally distressed but when the men of the party were informed, there was a buzz of interest. Most men are natural would-be plumbers and however incapable, they have their own theories. D and the Governor struggled out of their white dinner jackets and were to be seen upside down under mummy's basin with the chief engineer. Everybody had his own idea on how to retrieve the ring and although their efforts were unsuccessful, everybody agreed that it had all been most interesting and a lovely party, all so different. The Chief Doctor's wife was consoled with an extra liqueur and she then told us that she admittedly had two wedding rings, one gold, which was lost and one platinum, which she would wear the following day. The next morning Sammy the Indian foreman arrived with suitable grappling equipment. 'Lucky woman', he commented as the missing ring was retrieved.

After all these months of upheaval we were all thankful to wave goodbye to our smiling Chinese ladies who sent all their money back to their families in China. The lorries, the machinery, the bags of cement and the piles of wood were gone, and we were beginning to relax and feel the sense of peace returning. Unfortunately, the final departing lorry driver also had a feeling of release as he drove through the gate beside the guardhouse. He put his foot on the accelerator and knocked down the gatepost. Sammy's sad comment was, 'General very angry, Mem mad!'

My father decided it was all very well for me to do the flowers, to inspect the new kitchen and arrange the menus for my mother, but I really ought to be doing something useful and constructive as well. Singapore had a number of girls doing office jobs in various headquarters (unkindly, they were sometimes called the fishing fleet) and D thought I should have a secretarial training as well. My mother undertook to teach me how to type. She had taught a number of D's clerks in India and I believe she once stood a disruptive Sergeant in the corner. D's chief clerk would teach me shorthand. I was in an exclusive class of three and I was very fond of my classmates. Jane was the daughter of the Bishop of Bath and Wells and Noelle the wife of an English policeman attached to the Singapore police. D's chief clerk turned out to be a small dictator and all the injustices he had suffered from his domineering wife he took out on us so, it was quite hard going. Our one piece of light relief came when we were instructed to translate *Three Men in a Boat* into shorthand. Eventually I emerged as a far from competent secretary. My only attributes were honesty and a willingness to try.

My first job came when Robin Woods, the Archdeacon of Singapore, asked me to stand in for his secretary who was going on leave. Robin was later to become Dean of Windsor and Bishop of Worcester. I had a sort of loosebox behind the font and when a tropical Sumatra blew up, flakes of plaster would cover the typewriter from the ceiling. Robin on the other hand had an office the size of a broom cupboard behind the altar. We were all very friendly and we used to run up and down the aisle to each other. St Andrews Cathedral was largely open in the oppressive heat and we had chanting Indians and Malays and lost Chinese drifting in and out, and on one occasion a rabid dog, which had to be taken away by the dog catcher, poor creature.

I was very proud of the first letter I typed for Robin. He always chose brown typewriter ribbons and I had to copy a letter from the Bishop of Singapore. I managed to reach the bottom of the page without a single mistake but when I came to the signature, I was faced with a dilemma. The Bishop had signed himself 'Henry Singapore' with the sign of the Cross. I looked all around the typewriter keys but there was no adding sign, no multiplication sign, so in desperation I put down 'plus Henry.' I think the Woods family nicknamed him 'Plus Henry' ever after.

One morning Robin came into my office and said, 'June, I'm going up country for three weeks, will you send out the invitations for the opening of the Memorial Hall.' Robin, besides being a wonderful preacher and a very nice man, was also astute. He badly wanted a larger office and ideally committee rooms and meeting rooms for the Cathedral congregation, which represented all colours: white, yellow, brown and black. He had then discovered that the Far East had no War Memorial for those who died in the war, many in horrific circumstances. So the idea came about and the money flooded in from Hong Kong to Australia, so a very handsome Memorial Hall was built next to the Cathedral and it could be used by all denominations. All of this was very successful, but the invitations to the opening did not bear thinking about. The military hospital in Singapore did have its own memorial. It was a small organ in the hospital chapel, which was dedicated to the memory of those patients who had been bayoneted in their beds by the invading Japanese army.

I returned home for lunch with my parents and almost wept over my cottage pie. 'I don't know where to begin. There are all the Governors, the choir, the Mother's Union, and all the missionaries,' I cried. My father looked at me over his half glasses and remarked very kindly, 'I think old girl you had better hand this one over to me.' Robin totally unaware of what problems he had left behind him, was meanwhile making his way through the jungle in Malaya, while D delegated two staff officers to work on the project for a month. It was all a great success although there was no seat for me at the ceremonial opening, which was planned by D himself.

We were able to help the Woods family in another way. We'd all met on board ship travelling out to Singapore and they had been accompanied by a very sweet but rather plain cousin, whose job it was to help Ena with the large family of Woods children. The cousin Rosemary was about my age and knowing very few people, she often homed onto us on her days off. My mother regarded her as a challenge and we set about the task of transforming her like Eliza Doolittle. Her hair was shaped and curled, she was encouraged to wear a little makeup and her wardrobe was transformed, so we all felt proud and very happy when she became engaged to Robin's curate.

Fortunately for Robin, his very capable secretary returned from leave and I started to look for another job. I was accepted by the Navy to become PA to the Chief of Staff Far East Station. They did not enquire about my shorthand speed but they must have thought I was trustworthy; being D's daughter and unlikely to discuss the evacuation of Hong Kong at a cocktail party. It was all arranged on trust and apart from a lecture on not talking at parties, I never had to sign the Official Secrets Act, although I was in sole charge of all the top secret filing. My immediate boss who shared my office was a Lieutenant Commander who was delightful but distinctly vague. On one or two occasions he managed to set his waste paper basket on fire when he knocked his smouldering pipe out. One day I was sent to track down a certain top-secret pack, which had been borrowed by someone in headquarters and not returned. From room to room I went, 'Excuse me but do you have happened to have seen Pack PQS?' with no result. I returned to my boss empty-handed. 'Oh, who wants it June?' 'You do', I replied rather tartly.

I was delighted to show off my naval language to my parents, I did not file I logged my packs and if I dropped something on the floor, I must remember to call it the deck. On being driven home for lunch, one was taken by the Liberty boat. This was all great fun but I never achieved my ambition. No Wrens were allowed east of Suez so Rosemary G. and I did their jobs without the glamorous uniform, which I had always coveted. Rosemary G. was a sweet friend and she was a very capable PA to the Admiral but she was faced with a dilemma. She was very much in love with Brian, the Flag Lieutenant and he was undoubtedly devoted to her but he'd not yet proposed and her parents were destined to return to England in the near future. Poor Rosemary was much depressed. My parents tried to help by inviting her to stay on with us for some months as company for me. This was a very happy solution, but despite the fact that Rosemary had all the makings of a future Admiral's wife, Brian still never spoke of love. Then one day he invited her out sailing and Rosemary and I devised a plan that she was to tell him she was going to apply for a job in Australia. In the mean time, I ordered a special dinner. It was not wasted, Australia had fixed it, and a blissfully happy engaged couple returned to eat it and yes, many years later, Brian did make her an Admiral's wife.

Part of my job was to log all the signals that poured into the office, secret, top-secret and frantic. I was surprised to see that a consignment of rabbit meat was put on the top-secret list. I suppose frantic might intimate that they were passed sell by date. I found the logging of these signals sometimes overwhelming and faced with a tottering pile I transferred the lot onto the floor of Rosemary's office and laid them all out in a sort of fan. I thought that the offices were empty until the Admiral appeared behind me. 'Hello June, have you gone all Japanese?' My bosses were all very kind and great fun although I still dreaded being asked to collect my coffee cup from a crowded wardroom.

Unfortunately, our time in Singapore was rather overshadowed by my mother and I taking it in turns to go into hospital. The temperature seldom rose over ninety degrees but it was very humid and D did not take any leave for about two years. I still feel guilty admitting we were not very happy in Singapore, although life was pleasant and comfortable.

CHAPTER SEVEN

A Dakota and a Duchess

〜〜〜〜〜〜〜〜〜〜〜〜〜〜〜〜〜〜〜〜〜〜〜〜〜〜〜〜〜〜〜〜〜〜〜〜

We all loved the country, but we were restricted to spending most of our time on the island due to the bandit war being fought in Malaya. D eventually decided to take some fishing leave in Ceylon, or Sri Lanka as it is now called. The alternative was Hong Kong and that would have meant another urban existence. Our trip to Ceylon proved rather an anti-climax. We enjoyed the voyage on the troop ship with so many friends. When D had been asked on an official form the reason for his trip he put down 'fun'. When we landed at Colombo, we had quick impressions of that beautiful island; the dazzling colours of the women's saris, a flock of crows riding on the back of an open fruit cart behaving with all the noisy enthusiasm of a school outing and elephants having their daily bath in the river, before we zigzagged up the mountain road to the tea estate where we were to break our journey.

Our host was incredibly kind and it was a joy to sit by the wood fire in his charming bungalow and then walk around his garden filled with roses and English herbaceous plants. The last part of our journey had to be made by four-wheel drive vehicles and I often wonder whether D's very kind friend who had worked out the suggestions for our holiday had thought of the women of the party, and as it turned out one very sick woman, when it came to plans for our accommodation. The rest house turned out to be dark, cramped, and damp, and the cooking was horrendous. For a young fishing-mad bachelor it would have been adequate but it was far from ideal for someone like my mother, who had been suffering from a very painful leg from the start of our trip. I raided all the empty bedrooms in the rest house and managed to make my parents' room reasonably comfortable and I picked wild flowers for all the spare tooth glasses to cheer up their room. But the native staff refused to put on the lights until it was completely dark and in the meantime the leopards kept watch outside.

D had two days fishing after rainbow trout and I went with him for one magic jungle trek but the omens were not good. My mother never complained and she always said she would be better the following day, but her thrombosis as it turned out to be was not helped by living at 7,000 feet and D realised she must have medical help and the sooner the better. We were driven back to Colombo by a number of very kind friends and here the RAF took over. My mother had always sworn that she would never, never fly unless she was being rescued. The date was Friday the 13th but as we were all together we decided that it didn't matter and Mummy and I had our first flight from Colombo to Trincomalee in a Dakota. At Trincomalee we completed our journey back to Singapore by flying boat and I shall never forget the magic of that trip. The placid sea shimmered like the inside of a pearl and the golden beaches edged with palms surpassed anything a travel agent could envisage. We were the only passengers on board the flying boat and for five breath-taking minutes, I was allowed to sit at the controls. Since then I have never had any fear of flying and although it can sometimes be rather bumpy and even tedious, at its best one finds oneself in a world of pure magic and freedom.

My mother was rushed into hospital on our arrival in Singapore and she had to be there for several weeks during which time she tried unsuccessfully to give up smoking. She even asked one of the nurses to steal a cigarette from a sleeping officer on D's staff. This did not help but shortly afterwards when she returned home she announced to her unbelieving family that she was definitely giving up. She did, and she never looked back. It is hard to imagine how my parents lived into old age when they were virtually chain smokers in their youth, but for their generation, it was never considered to be dangerous. Fortunately, I have never liked smoking and I certainly dislike the smell of a smoke filled room although I always found Jimmy's pipe smoke comforting.

In 1952 Singapore received an official visit from Princess Marina, HRH the Duchess of Kent and her son who was about to celebrate his seventeenth birthday. All three services were to entertain the royal visitors for one day each and there was to be a ball, a birthday party, garden parties and all kinds of excitements. Certainly among the senior ladies who were to act as hostesses there were only two topics of conversation. What shall we wear and what shall we give her to eat? D solved the problem of entertaining the young Duke for one day by instructing his most imaginative young officer to conduct him round the army dog section. The dogs had been recruited either to guard or to sniff out bandits and other unwanted personnel. This was followed by an afternoon let loose with the bulldozers. These huge machines were deployed to level a large section of land destined to become a new camp, and goodness knows how long it took the engineers afterwards to 'undo' this huge sand castle venture. But later that day just as the national anthem struck up and Princess Marina stepped out of Government House into the grounds to greet her guests, two very dirty, slightly shame-faced individuals slipped in by the back door of Government House after an extremely happy afternoon.

Una Slim was living with us at this time and she and I were honoured to receive invitations to the Governor's dinner, to celebrate the young Duke's seventeenth birthday. It was to be a Chinese meal for twenty, eaten with chopsticks, and after dinner a number of other young people would arrive to dance. I still think it was probably the most unnerving dinner I have ever eaten. I was seated on the Governor's left and Princess Marina was on his right. Una was seated on the other side of the table on the Duke's left and Viscount Althorp (later to become Earl Spencer) was on her left. The Governor was a very gentle, kind man who had had great sadness in his private life.

But chopsticks seemed cruelty to animals. I think I once tried to use chopsticks but they do need practice, and it was rather like being called on to use knitting needles. Fortunately my companion on my left, Mr. Phillip Haye who was part of the Princess's entourage was charming and very forgiving of my attempts, but I feel it would have been kind if they had said. 'Well you have all done your best, you may now use a spoon.' After dinner, we all moved into another room and an impressive birthday cake was wheeled in blazing with candles. The young Duke attempted to blow them out but was stopped by a violent protest from the other guests. 'No, no, he must slice the candles out with the kukri knife the Gurkhas gave him, when he was in Malaya. The kukri was presented to him and he made a dashing forehand drive at the cake. The candles were extinguished but there was a horrified silence when we saw that he had accidentally caught the corner of his mother's eye with the knife and blood was pouring down her beautiful dress. She proved then that she was not only charming and beautiful but also very brave. 'Carry on, carry on, everybody', she said as she left the room to change. It was merciful that her eye was not damaged but she developed a very black eye and over the rest of her visit she was extra skilful with her makeup and frequently wore dark glasses.

Una had become engaged to Nigel Fraser, General Templer's ADC, while she was staying with us and she was soon to return to England for her wedding. I too was in a state of excitement for her mother Aileen Slim, wife of Field Marshall Sir William Slim, invited me to go to Australia to become her personal assistant and lady in waiting. Bill Slim was then representing the Queen as Governor General. Once again clothes seemed the top priority for I was to arrive a few days before the official visit of the Queen and the Duke of Edinburgh.

Luckily I was not destined to take up my official duties until after the royal visit but I could shadow Judy Hutchinson my predecessor.

A few weeks before I left Singapore for Australia I had my appendix removed in the military hospital, but by the day of my departure I was reasonably fit again. I had mixed feelings about the whole adventure. I was very proud to have been invited to take up such a post but rather anxious about what it would involve. I hated the idea of leaving my mother and father, but I knew they were thrilled for me to have this opportunity and after all, I was not going to be amongst strangers, but with old friends of my parents. I don't think I have ever been ambitious, but I was determined to do my best and try not to let anyone down. Preparing for a new job in a new environment was always going to be a challenge but to arrive about a fortnight before the visit of the first reigning Monarch to visit Australia was bound to make everything fairly traumatic.

CHAPTER EIGHT

In Waiting

Government House was a large, gracious house set in the midst of a beautiful garden with sweeping lawns and mature trees, herbaceous borders and an awesome view of the Blue Mountains. It was invigorating to be back in a climate, which was like an ideal English summer with none of the stickiness of the tropics. One of my first tasks was to get to know the other members of Government House staff. The Controller was Commander John Griffin, Royal Australian Navy. The Military Secretary Lieutenant Colonel Martin Gilliat was a loveable man with an impish sense of humour and a remarkable war record, which included several escapes as a POW. He went on to work for

1954 Government House Canberra

the Queen Mother after he left Government House. The three ADCs were Lieut – Commander Bob Brokenshire, Australian Navy; Major John Swinton, Scots Guards, ex Harrovian who had lost a leg in the war; and Squadron Leader Jeff Blackwell, Royal Australian Airforce, perhaps the most thoughtful member of staff. In addition, there was Murray Tyrell, the official Secretary who lived with his sweet wife Nell in a little house in the grounds.

I also had to find my way about the house. On the ground floor, Government House had one very long reception room, a large dining room, a smaller morning room, Uncle Bill's study and, tucked away around the corner of the end of the hall, there were the ADC's office, Martin's office and mine. The typist pool was housed in a small extension. Upstairs Aileen and Bill had their own bedroom and dressing room and she had a charming sitting room overlooking the garden. Naturally, the arrival of the Queen and the Duke meant that everyone had to move one down in bedroom priorities and for the duration of the Queen's visit I slept at the Prime Minister's lodge, being collected at 6:45 a.m. to help with the flowers. In spite of months of planning, the last minute preparations were extensive and having to plan the various receptions and investitures it would have been a great advantage to have had a revolving stage. As it was, we all became as competent as Pickfords at removing and re-arranging the furniture. In my letter to my parents, I tried to describe this frenzied activity. 'The grounds are full of police, boy scouts, and troops rehearsing for a ceremonial parade, and the house is full of electricians and cinema operators.' The royal party was to be entertained in the evening by a film and this involved importing a complete cinema apparatus weighing one and a half tons. Three floorboards had collapsed under the strain and all the cinema operators from the local cinema had moved into the house, leaving the usherettes to run the local cinema for a week. Round every corner, one would run into those irreplaceable supports of a free country, the committee, and the conference.

Numerous parcels would arrive throughout the day; lamp standards, cushions, bedspreads, a white cloth for the investiture and a full-grown lamb for the kitchen.

I have often thought that the Ministry of Works, or whichever department has the responsibility for furnishing official residences, shows very little imagination. In every case, the occupant has to entertain and 'show the flag' and it is difficult to make a house gracious when you are unable to call on old family furniture and pictures. The Ambassador or General, or more often their wives, have to do the best they can, but it is not always the best way to show off to foreign dignitaries. There must be so many sources that a government department can call upon to make an official residence really elegant, so many pictures stacked away in museums that never see the light of day.

D was eventually given a new car in Germany, after he had been watched by the entire Diplomatic Corps, helping to push his old Humber down the drive after attending an official party. I think the Americans do this far better and their Embassies are really delightful and furnished in perfect taste. The American Embassy in Canberra was most attractive and only just completed in the early 50s. I believe it is an exact replica of the Governor's residence in Williamsburg. Washington had insisted that it should be identical to that residence but the first Ambassador insisted on having a sunroom added as well. Washington replied that Williamsburg did not have a sunroom, so why should it be necessary. The struggle went on for some time and finally the Ambassador said, 'OK you fellows, if that's the way you want it, but if you don't give me my sunroom I shall dress like the Governor of Williamsburg did then, knee breeches and all!'

He got it.

In addition to all these parcels, dresses were sent out from London for Aileen. Aileen was a perfectionist and fastidious and when it came to her clothes she tended to be extravagant and ruthless, attacking twenty guinea hats (remember this was the 50s), and tearing off feathers and veiling with the abandon of a bargain hunter at a jumble sale. Hundred guinea dresses were dismissed as being 'just not her', which meant a considerable amount of repacking and reordering. But there were many funny moments. I discovered Martin in his vest and underpants standing in the passage with the telephone in his hands saying, 'Yes we are definitely wearing whites,' and the poor workman who pinched his finger and was hopping around on one foot received no sympathy from his foreman. 'That's alright man, you'll get compensation.'

Naturally I called Uncle Bill 'Your Excellency' from now on, and he was very willing to help, but his bright ideas could have disastrous effects when he introduced the wrong stool or chair into the drawing room or tried to hang another picture in the Duke's bedroom. His attempts to rally the teams of new Australians working on the awnings outside were equally unhelpful. At this time new Australians tended to come from Holland, Poland or Yorkshire, but the team putting up the awnings outside the Queen's room were Polish and were chatting away in their own language when Uncle B came along and said, 'Hi you chaps, you're Australian now. Talk Australian!' with the result that they got into a most awful bother, because every time one wanted a hammer his mate handed him a chisel. In the end Uncle Bill had to leave them to it. But everyone agreed that it would be unwise to allow the troops from Papaya to move the cinema apparatus, because it would probably end up in the bathroom.

There was one unfortunate incident, which fortunately has never reached the headlines. Two days before the royal party arrived, Susie, Aileen's wirehaired fox terrier was discovered to have ringworm. This was horrendous news indeed. Ringworm, and the Queen was about to get into her bed labelled: Susie Slept Here! There was nowhere to send the little dog, so she would have to be incarcerated in Aileen's bathroom and only exercised by Uncle Bill and myself. The entire household, and the royal staff would be told that she was in season. Needless to say, that the blankets on the royal bed would be changed. After all the planning, it was hard to take it in when the official visit to Canberra actually began.

Judy, my predecessor, and I had been down to Sydney to see the *Gothic* arrive, but now the Queen was coming to us to stay in her own official residence. We staff were all lined up in the hall to greet them. Uncle Bill and Aileen presented us, first to HM and then the Duke. After nearly half a century it may be hard for some people to appreciate how lovely the Queen was as a young woman; petite and dainty with a dazzling complexion and an inward beauty that made itself felt to all who came in contact with her. Dame Pattie Menzies told me that hardened members of the opposition who had not spoken to her for years came to her with tears in their eyes saying, 'isn't she lovely?'

On that first evening, it was a family party with just the two staffs and there was much laughter because a lot of the luggage had not arrived. All the papers and office equipment had turned up and HM had said, 'Who would mind if that was lost?' But there were no evening shoes and bags for the ladies in waiting, so Lady Pamela Mountbatten had to wear her dark blue and white court shoes under her evening dress. I could not help her, as her feet were two sizes smaller than mine. I lent Lady Alice Edgerton a nightdress but she did not need it because her luggage arrived after dinner. Aileen took me to sit with the Queen after dinner and she was so easy and kind and apparently much amused when I admitted I had never had a test for my new appointment. The Queen and the Duke went to bed early but Judy, Martin, John Swinton and I took about three of the royal staff off to an Elizabethan Ball at a hotel in Canberra. It was fun but I don't think I ever had more tired feet.

We returned to Government House about one o'clock and I changed into my frock for the morning in Judy's room. Kind Jeff lent me his alarm clock and I was whisked off to the Prime Minister's lodge in an official car with a Boy Scout sitting in front to guide the driver. All went well and the car and the Boy Scout left me safely on the Menzies' doorstep and disappeared into the night, and then I discovered I could not get in. Dame Pattie had promised that she would leave the door open for me because they could not find the spare key and I just had to walk up to my room. However, they were still at the dance and in their hurry to leave the house they must have forgotten. I remember thinking at the time: "I'm sure this will never happen to me again. I'm sitting on the doorstep of the Prime Minister of Australia at half past one in the morning with an alarm clock in one hand, an airbag on my shoulder, and my kimono dressing gown over my arm, having dined with the Queen earlier this evening." The whole situation was ludicrous, but fortunately I found help from the policeman at the lodge gate, who somehow found a way in via the back regions. In the morning I dared not use the bathroom they had allotted me because the Prime Minister slept with his door open directly next door and I should have been loath to disturb the even flow of senatorial snores that floated down the passage.

Arriving at Government House, Judy and I crept upstairs to rescue the flowers from the passage of the royal suite. Mrs Instone, a charming professional decorator from Sydney had also arrived and we worked furiously until 10:30 am to finish them all in time. Mrs Instone and I became great friends and it was a delight to work with a professional florist for the first time, for she could teach me so much. She did most of the big arrangements downstairs and Judy and I shared HM's room and the Duke's room upstairs. I gather from my letters to my parents that I had to dine alone with eight men that evening, as the Queen and the Duke were dining with the Menzies. Aileen had gone to bed and Judy had taken Pamela off to a party in

Canberra. My comment was, 'I'm getting quite used to this situation and it can be very entertaining, as men are always more interesting when they talk among themselves.'

When the Queen opened Parliament in Canberra she wore her Coronation dress and Norman Hartnell had never designed anything more beautiful. Every fold was encrusted with embroidery in soft mother of pearl colouring. The colours were so soft they seemed to enhance her own colouring and she very thoughtfully walked up and down the hall to show off the dress to all the maids.

During my time at Government House I was constantly brought back to reality by Susie. There was a time she chewed my best petticoat, my ancient teddy bear that always sat on my bed and *My Daily Strength for Daily Needs*. She had obviously read the title. There was a time I was having a dress fitted in my bedroom and I was appalled to discover she'd picked up a small gold safety pin which was opened and was within two centimetres of her throat and there was the occasion when she chose to roll in something unspeakable a few hours before the arrival of Lord and Lady Attlee to stay. I can only think it must have been fox because two baths in my bathroom with scented soap appeared to make little difference and finally with one eye on the clock I tipped my bottle of Elizabeth Arden's Bluegrass all over her. Fox added to Bluegrass is unforgettable and the ADCs were stunned when they encountered her. But poor Lady Attlee also had her troubles, because she knocked over a silver inkstand on a very narrow writing table in her bedroom and ink poured down the wall and over the carpet.

My days at Government House invariably began at 7 am and ended well after midnight. Besides acting as nanny to Susie, I arranged all the flowers and at times this amounted to twenty-eight vases. I also dealt with all Aileen's correspondence and together with one of the ADCs I arranged her future engagements for visiting and sometimes wrote her speeches. I was responsible for entertaining and cosseting all the female guests and I think we must have made an official visit to one of the other states about once a month. But I was very lucky to see something of all the states; New South Wales, Victoria, Queensland, Western Australia, Southern Australia and the northern territories as well as Tasmania. It was all incredibly interesting but I always wished there was more time to take everything in without having to be ruled by my watch. I once asked Sir Richard Colville if he ever got used to the pace of royal visits, which he helped to arrange and he replied, 'No, never. I always get butterflies.'

Whenever we had an official dinner party, I kept two pairs of my long white washable gloves on my bed to hand to some unfortunate lady guest who had either forgotten her gloves or did not realise we always wore them in the evenings. Some women became very agitated at the thought of doing the wrong thing or wearing something unsuitable and I remember being called out of my bath, wrapped only in a towel, to advise an agitated women who wanted to know if she should curtsey when Aileen sat in front of her in church. I really did not know the answer myself but I always followed the rule of, if in doubt, curtsey.

We had one entertaining dinner party when an exceedingly pretty grazier's daughter was electrified to find a large unknown insect had disappeared down the front of her dress at the dinner table. I smuggled her out through the pantry and helped to rescue her but that was not the end of the party. I had arranged a lot of golden rod in the arrangements in the drawing room and poor Jan took one sniff and was overcome with hay fever. The only solution was to remove all the vases containing golden rod and place them in a row in the garden.

We met so many interesting people who either stayed of attended the various functions; politicians, diplomats, heads of services, captains of industry, artists, writers, musicians, bishops, graziers, sportsmen. One lady guest solved her dress problem by wearing a beautifully cut perfectly plain black dress with various changes of jewellery, so she had pearls for breakfast, diamonds for lunch and some fabulous emeralds for the evening. How snobby can you be? One evening we had a reception at Admiralty House in Sydney and I discovered a quiet, rather lost little man standing in a corner with nothing to drink and no one to talk to. I asked him his name and he just said Nuffield. No one except Uncle Bill had known he was coming and he had not told the staff. I could not have been more astonished if I'd discovered the Archbishop of Canterbury hiding behind a door.

But life was not all tiaras and turtle soup. There were so very many funny, touching, poignant occasions where our hosts had tried so desperately hard to mount a solemn occasion and it somehow got lost along the way. The first time I accompanied Aileen was when she was invited to inspect a rally of Guides and Brownies just outside Canberra. I had made a recce before and we were rather concerned that the organisers had only just thought of engaging a band two days before Aileen's visit. Needless to say, the band did not materialise and we had to endure music from an extremely ancient gramophone, which became more and more tired. I had to force myself not to rush out and wind it up. The Brownies were lined up as a guard of honour in a distant part of the field and Aileen then had to watch a march past by the Guides who might have come straight out of a St. Trinian's film. Short blue uniforms, scraped back hair, tummies sticking out. They were so serious and so gallant, but I shall never again feel the same about the march of the gladiators. One girl appeared to be marching in great pain and her company leader told me that she was wearing shoes two sizes too small for her and then she added, by explanation, there are a lot in her family. After the march past and Aileen's speech, the gramophone was turned off and we all sang 'the Queen' in various tones and pitches of discord.

On another recce to a small township out in the bush, Jeff and I had to try to help the organisers prop up the piano when one of the legs fell off. There was great consternation in one township when, a few days before the visit of the Governor General and his wife, they discovered that half their cups and saucers were missing in their small hall. A guard was mounted all night in the hope of catching the thieves and they then discovered that in fact, no china was missing; they just miscounted.

Shortly after the end of the royal tour, Aileen and Uncle Bill were invited to stay on board the cruiser HMAS Australia when she took her last cruise up the barrier reef before she went to the breaking yards. Our party included Martin, Bob and myself and Johnson, Uncle Bill's valet. We went aboard in the shadow of Sydney Bridge, a glorious sunset turning the sky every shade of yellow and flame and as we were piped aboard. Aileen and I had our first battle of the skirts. Looking back, I cannot imagine why we did not wear trousers throughout our time on board but it may not have been considered proper in the 50s. I wrote to my parents:

'On Sunday we had a service on the quarterdeck; hats and alas skirts and oh dear I have never had such a battle. Aileen had very wisely worn a dress with a double skirt, which being fairly heavy was reasonably controlled but mine was taking off like a loose jib. Fortunately, it was a short service. No hymns because the padre insists on playing his squeeze-box and it drives the captain mad, but Uncle Bill read the lesson and we all listened to a rather tedious sermon from the padre. Oh dear what lack of imagination these padres have. Imagine preaching on honesty is the best policy when you're standing on the deck with a bright sun flashing on the white horses on the sea and the spray cutting away from our wash behind us and everything is as bright, and fresh and as wonderful as God can make it and you just want to say lift up your eyes and thank God. However, it was hard to concentrate anyway because my skirt was going crack, flop, flap, like a flyaway kite. There was Martin whispering, "Hold on old girl, not* *much longer," and all the officers lined up behind us; definitely not my finest hour. But they all said I managed quite neatly.'*

Our quarters were in the cuddy or Admiral's quarters. They were directly aft, which meant we had our own sitting room and dining room. The former came to a point at one end proving one could go no further. In this, there was a gold-framed reproduction of a painting of Nelson. Aileen had what was normally the Admiral's cabin and I had the Flag Lieutenant's. We shared a bathroom and the greatest thrill was to have a soft water bath.

It was rather exciting to feel that we were making history as we discovered we were the first women to travel in one of her Majesty's Australian ships since 1935 when the Duchess of York, as she was then, travelled out to Australia with the Duke. It was an exhilarating trip, but rather a sad one, for in the end the old ship was to be broken up. I cannot remember where it was but we passed the inlet where other ships were already being attacked by the breakers men. Partly dismantled and covered with rust it was a tragic sight like

1954 HMAS Australia – the battle of the skirts!

some elephant's graveyard. I think Hamlet would have known how to describe it.

The Navy have always been superlative hosts and we were really spoilt, our little steward even caught special fish for our breakfast. But the most delightful of all was our host. Captain Alan McNicoll, Royal Australian Navy, had been awarded the George Medal in the war. Tall and ruggedly ugly he had the most charming courtly manners. He was a scholar, was very interested in painting and wrote charming little poems for his children. All this with a great sense of humour, so I very nearly lost my heart. On the voyage we met all the officers in the wardroom, for different men would join us for lunch or dinner every day. On our second day of the voyage we joined Uncle Bill on the bridge to see the eight-inch guns fired for the last time. Even with cotton wool in our ears, we jumped at every broadside; the impact was stupendous.

After the second day, we started to cruise in among the various islands. We anchored off one called Pine Island, where three families lived and tended the lighthouse. They had received our signal to say we were coming ashore only about two hours before, so they must have had a rush to be ready to receive us. All three husbands were there to greet us on the rocks that formed a tiny jetty. We clambered from the launch to a dingy and then on to the rocks up some wooden steps up the side of the cliffs. It was all completely different to what I expected a Pacific island to be. There were very few palms but a great number of pine trees combined with semi-tropical flowers and exotic butterflies. The lighthouse was perched on the top of the cliff, gaily painted white with a red roof. It was quite a stiff climb to reach it and Aileen and I preferred to stay down at the bottom while the men folk all went up to the light.

I discovered then that I could feel as giddy looking up at the high tower as I would if I looked down from a great height and I was grateful to stay where I was because I never liked spiral staircases.

After that we went down to one of the three little houses and were given tea. It was an occasion for celebration, for it was the sixteenth wedding anniversary for one of the families. It was all delightfully informal and cheerful sitting round their kitchen table while the children played at our feet. The sun was setting as we left them and the lamp had been lit. We had a terrific send-off and as the launch sped over the calm sea in the path of the setting sun, we waved and waved until they vanished from our sight and only the twinkling light of the lighthouse was left to guide us home.

We laid anchor that night and next morning we set sail for the group of islands called after Sir James Smith. They had enchanting names; Goldsmith, Silversmith, Anvil – anything to do with a smithy. We went ashore at Goldsmith Island and it was an idyllic spot; a golden sandy beach, perfect for bathing, framed by grey volcanic rocks. Above, dipping down to the beach itself, were thick woods of pine and semi-tropical trees with flocks of white cockatoos and bright butterflies flitting amongst the branches. It was a perfect setting for *the Tempest*, with Martin our own winsome Ariel.

That night we were dined out in the wardroom. I believe only one woman had been dined out in an Australian wardroom since the war, so we made it three and once again felt we were making history. We always drank the Queen's health every night and it felt very strange to drink it sitting down. The next day we visited another island to bathe and have a gigantic picnic.

The worst part of our return trips was when we mounted the gangway, covered in sand and feeling as if we had been pulled through a hedge backwards, to be greeted by an immaculate reception committee of officers and ratings, all rigidly at attention. But they were very sweet and most of them grinned as they saluted.

We had one 'trippery' day, calling at Hayman Island, which was rather like a glorified Butlins, bringing holidaymakers to the island about twice a week by flying boat. It was all there – the chalets, the swimming pool, the housey-housey and all. The following day, after a huge picnic, we were helped into a glass-bottomed boat and Alan McNicoll and one of his officers rowed us over some of the reefs to look at the coral. I never admitted it, but I was a little disappointed, as I had expected the coral to be bright pink, just like the necklace I was given as a child, but this coral appeared to be mostly a dirty grey with patches of yellow. However, the shapes were beautiful and it was fascinating to see the sea urchins and little fish in their natural environment. We were lucky enough to borrow the same glass-bottom boat that the Queen had used.

The following morning I woke at three a.m., to discover we were under way again, and not only under way but going flat out. Living directly over the screw, our cabins were shaken to pieces and you could hardly speak for the rattle and clatter. We had been expecting to land at Townsville later that day, but it appeared that during the night the ship had received a signal to say a Dutch tank landing ship had broken down with only half an engine and was drifting towards the reef. The men in the Dutch ship were not in danger of losing their lives but their ship could well have been lost on the reef. Ours was the only ship in the vicinity and we were racing to the rescue. Uncle Bill was determined to see the rescue, even though it was going to confuse our schedule at Government House where various guests were arriving to stay.

We had a semi-buffet lunch in Uncle Bill's cabin, which was rather less shaky than the other day cabin, but even as we rattled and banged about it was as if we were in a runaway train, and they chose that day to give us spaghetti. All day we kept at full speed and, as we got out into the open water of the Coral Sea, it was fairly heavy going for we were rolling and heaving as well. About teatime, they sent out a Sunderland plane to help us in our search for the Dutchmen and messages went backward and forwards as it circled over our heads. 'Good hunting,' 'That makes two of us.' Darkness fell and we had had no further message from the LCT since early that morning. Aileen and I were feeling slightly uppity inside for it was very hot with our cabins battened down and then Johnson filled Uncle Bill's bath too full and there was a minor flood. But just as we were sitting down to dinner, a signal came through and we were all set for sighting the LCT about 10:30 p.m.

It was a fairly stormy night with a strong trade wind blowing and dark clouds hiding the moon, but it was a wonderful moment when far ahead we sighted the lights of the LCT. Poor things, the Dutchmen had been rolling and floundering away for about four days and I'm sure they must have been thankful to see our lights too. Aileen, Uncle Bill, Martin, Bob and I clambered up to the little platform just below the bridge. Aileen and I were feeling pretty proud of ourselves on these swaying ladders in the dark and we had a grandstand view of the whole operation. We took much longer to come alongside than I would have thought, I suppose because the seas were very rough and we were frightened of a collision, but eventually we got about half a length ahead of her. They first of all tried floating the line back to her on a life buoy but that went adrift, so they fired it across and at the third attempt the Dutchmen caught it. First there was a thin cord, then a thick rope and finally the steel cable. We had about three hundred National Service trainees on board so it was easier for us to manhandle the cables; but for the ten or so Dutchmen tossing and heaving on a spray-swept deck, it was a different proposition. They could not get our cable across so in the end we took about half of theirs and attached it to ours. All this took hours and when Aileen and Bill and I went to bed about 1:30, they were still at it. I believe we took them in tow about 2:30 a.m. We should have made four knots but because of the wind and the tide, we only made about one knot for fear of the towrope breaking. We eventually towed them into Cairns and, as we cast them off the entire Dutch crew was standing on their deck in immaculately clean uniforms to salute Uncle Bill. It was a very moving moment.

Throughout my time in Australia, the weekly diary was always filled with various happenings and it's hard to choose which were the most memorable. Our visit to the Flying Doctor's headquarters at Alice Springs was certainly one. That and our brief participation in the School of the Air for children in widely dispersed parts of the outback. But I shall certainly never forget our visit to an Aborigine settlement. An elderly man greeted us and Aileen and I were each presented with a very pretty rush basket, which he had woven himself. He looked lost and unhappy, rather like a stray dog at the Battersea Dog's Home, with sad eyes that held no hope. I am speaking of life fifty years ago, and I am sure things must have improved for those ancient people by now. At the time I had to remind myself that if you are carving out a country and conditions are far from easy, survival and self-interest invariably come first. And it may take two or three generations who have gained in experience and found security to show compassion for a problem right under their noses. Looking back on our own historical past, we are far from blameless. I liked the Australians immensely. They were natural and brave and friendly, but it did make me sad to see their rather insensitive attitude to the Aborigines and for the animals in their care.

I clearly recall the visit of Sybil Thorndyke and her husband Sir Lewis Casson. She was enchanting but she never stopped acting and every time she glanced out of the window she would murmur, 'Oh those blue, blue hills.' We staff, the boys and myself showed off our party piece *Green Grow the Rushes Oh* and she helped to coach us in extra actions. But when I sat next to Sir Lewis at lunch, I found him rather heavy going because from the soup to the cheese he proceeded to describe to me the inner workings of a Rolls Royce engine. I tried to vary my replies, 'Really,' 'How interesting,' but it was difficult.

CHAPTER NINE

Re-Enter Jimmy

~~~~~~~~~~~~~~~~~~~~~~~~~~~~~~~~~~~~

My time at Government House was certainly a great experience, but I was glad to return home to England after eighteen months. The pace of our existence and the fact that for several months after my arrival I never had a day off, do bring about a build-up of tiredness and I longed to see my parents again. On my arrival home I tried for a job in London, but potential employers were not interested in my experience, only my shorthand speed. Then a kind friend suggested I go for an interview to become a kind of guide at some Ideal Home Exhibition. In order to be accepted, I would have to take an intelligence test.

I believe I never lost my head in my other jobs and I was quite calm when I discovered a large poisonous snake curled up on the mat just outside my office door in Canberra and when we suffered a minor earthquake shock, which opened up a wide crevasse just outside the front door. But faced with a stern woman with a stopwatch and a paper, which included questions like: If Tom is on the left of Bill and Bill was on the right of Charles who was in the middle? I developed mental paralysis and I was not accepted.

I was accepted by a small firm in Palace Street who were fairly easy going about my shorthand and were busy promoting Hopalong Cassidy. By running the Hopalong Cassidy fan club I added to my pay packet and I had great fun sending a large signed photograph of Hopalong Cassidy on his horse to one of my parent's oldest friends in Scotland. Major-General Sir Aymer Maxwell who was a Royal Archer and Deputy-Lieutenant had a signed photograph with, 'Hiya Partner, Your Old Friend Hoppy.'

I was very lucky to find a bed-sit in Ebury Street. One of my girlfriends had a room on the first floor and my room was at the top of the house, which proudly displayed a blue plaque, George Moore Lived Here. My landlady, Grace, was an elfin creature, fastidious and very kind and she worked for Harpers Bazaar. My room was light and airy, which was just as well, because Grace had papered one wall in black wallpaper with dashes of white like chalk scribbles on a blackboard. Grace was a perfectionist and when she gave a dinner party, it took about twenty-four hours to tackle the washing up. She was also a keen gardener and I could hardly bear to look when, dressed in diminutive shorts, she stepped out over London from her kitchen window on the top floor to attend to her various window boxes. Admittedly they were very pretty but I never relaxed until she was safely back in the kitchen.

Every Sunday evening, I would return from spending the weekend with my parents in Bedfordshire and bring a large bunch of flowers from D's lovely garden with me. Seeing an arrangement I had done, Grace exclaimed, 'June you should be working with flowers, I know a friend who works for Constance Spry. I will see if they have a vacancy.' Mercifully Constance Spry did not require an intelligence test and I became one of her five decorators. I remember my surprise when I first set eyes on the basement where we all worked. Hanging up on a clothes line amongst bunches of drying hydrangea was a pair of man's bathing trunks. I discovered that these belonged to a Mr. Price who bought all our flowers at Covent Garden. Every morning after he completed his marketing he would go for an icy dip in the Serpentine.

We decorators all had our own commissions for the week and after that we could be called to arrange flowers for a wedding, or a ball or some private individual. I was given the task of arranging the flowers in a big restaurant in Piccadilly, as well as the offices of Air India, a court photographer and St. Mary's Hospital. The res-

1956 Flower arranging with Constance Spry – avoiding certain individuals!

taurant was a rather thankless task, because the combination of heat and cigarette smoke was not ideal if you were trying to keep the flowers going for a week. Like any other job, I found myself avoiding certain individuals like the manager and the equally oily barman on the first floor, while counting the chef and Doris, who had the task of washing up the glasses, as my friends. One of the waiters with a spiteful nature put a broken wine glass in her washing up water and I slipped out to buy her some sticking plaster.

When Jimmy and I were married, she wrote to tell me that she could offer us a bed anytime we wanted to stay in London for she had a basement flat in St. George's Square. I was also invited to bring my fiancée to the restaurant for dinner on the house, but having an intimate knowledge of the kitchen, I never took the offer up. I imagine the kitchen inspections were not so strict in the 50s and having seen the floor thick with congealed grease and side-stepped the waste bins which had not been emptied for days, I was sure Jimmy would agree that bread and cheese would be preferable.

When I cleared the dead flowers away after the Christmas holidays, I would frequently go up to the street to inhale some semi-fresh air for the smell was really horrendous. St. Mary's was really our poor relation, because they could not afford many flowers and I would beg a few extra from the other decorators. I had to make an arrangement in the entrance hall, two in the nurses' dining room, two in the casualty ward and one in the waiting room. The housekeeper in the nurses' dining room was another friend and apart from giving me a cup of tea, she allowed me to take a cup to a patient in the waiting room who appeared to be recovering from cancer treatment and looked desperately ill. The porters were always teasing me and on the day I was expecting Jimmy to call for me so that we could choose my engagement ring together I remarked to Bill the head porter, 'I am expecting a friend to call for me, will you tell him I won't keep him long.' 'Him,' exclaimed Bill. 'A man!' He was one of the first to see my ring.

One of our most exciting contracts was decorating the extension to the Baltic Exchange, which was to be opened by the Queen. Every decorator past and present was called in but being the newest entry, I was sent all over the West End with the apprentice to touch-up the vases and make sure they had enough water. We then reported to the Baltic Exchange and I was a little taken aback when my boss said, 'Oh, there you are, June, you can arrange the five dolphins for the Queen's dining room.' A dolphin is a charming vase in the shape of a dolphin balancing a shell on its tail. It is a case of up one side and sweep down on the other side, not difficult but I wished I could have had a trial run first. However, all went well and they really did look very pretty filled with crimson roses and lavender.

We often did the flowers for No.10 and No.11 Downing Street. The Chancellor had an adorable yellow Labrador who used to pick up my bunches of flowers and carry them round in his mouth. I missed him when he was sent to live in the country, but London is not ideal for any dog. I also arranged the flowers for various shops in Bond Street. Mallets displayed the most exquisite antique furniture and one of our decorators had caused quite a sensation by arranging a charming bowl of dandelions on a walnut bureau. I made my mark quite literally by overfilling a vase and leaving a yellow ring on a very valuable table. I was appalled when I discovered my fault, but the French polisher dealt with it in seconds. Lancaster House, the

Opera House, Westminster Abbey and the Fishmonger's Hall, it was a joy to arrange the flowers in all these places, but I found there were some houses or buildings where I felt happy and relaxed and some that made me jumpy and uncomfortable although I never met the owners. Whether this atmosphere came from the present occupants or whether it reflected something or someone who had lived there in the past I never discovered, but I know I was very much aware of happiness or discord in the various places I visited.

I loved working for Constance Spry, but the pay was not good and there was very little over by the end of the week however much I cut down on food. I did try to earn a little extra by washing up for an Italian restaurant. One of the waitresses hurrying into the kitchen with a pile of dirty china whispered, 'Hush, I'm an actress.' But having filled my sink with clean soapy water, I was preparing to start on the pile when up from the basement appeared the Italian granny carrying a small bambino. Her eyes glistened when she saw my bubbling water and she proceeded to give the baby a luxurious bath. After she had dried him on a clean tea towel I removed the plug and started again.

But what about Jimmy you may be wondering. I was still working for Hopalong Cassidy when I decided to take a bus in my lunch hour and visit Swan and Edgar to buy some yellow gloves. Now I find it hard to believe I ever wanted yellow gloves, but at that time, I must have had a Malvolio complex and thought they would go with some outfit. But my guardian angel had been busy that morning and as I was boarding the bus the first person I bumped into was Jimmy's father Uncle Ronald, who was on his way to a Hepburn Starey Blind meeting with his secretary. I asked after Auntie Molly, I asked after Uncle Jack, I asked after Jimmy's sister Margaret and feeling it would be rather pointed if I left out Jimmy, I asked after him too. Within twenty-four hours, 'Dad' had written to Jimmy in Malta and reported that I had enquired after him.

The result was that I received a letter from Jimmy himself, asking me to dine with him when he returned home. That January, most of the country was blanketed in thick fog. I know Jimmy had a wretched journey to Woolwich from the docks, for all his vehicles had been deck cargo from Malta and not surprisingly, they had flat batteries. In the meantime, I was making my way around the West End trying to rescue flowers, which were dying while we looked at them. I must have picked up a bug too, because our first date had to be postponed. I remember saying to Mummy, ' I know he'll never believe I've been ill.' However, it was arranged that we should meet for dinner at his club, The Rag, on 31 January. My mother had said, 'You really must make up your mind now darling,' and I was in a state, which the Navy would have been correct in describing as frantic. I remember having my hair done and taking a taxi.

Unfortunately, everything had worked out so smoothly I was about to be far too early, so I paid the taxi to drive round and round Piccadilly Circus to lose time.

I have always firmly believed in prayer and that day I had prayed desperately that I should know what to decide. Jimmy was waiting to greet me and in one flash, I knew that I would never be happy unless I married him. We had an excellent dinner, talked about old times and the family, we may have even mentioned the weather but nothing of a more personal nature, and I felt I must take the initiative. That day Jimmy had bought three charming old prints of the Crimea from his club: 'The Battles of the Alma', 'The Battle of Inkerman' and 'The Charge of the Light Brigade'. He stacked them in front of us in the taxi in which he took me back to Ebury Street and feeling I could not leave the situation in a vacuum, I summoned up all my courage and asked, 'Why did you want to meet me again?' The reply was almost matter of fact, 'Well, I still loved you.' With that I put out my foot and the 'The Charge of the Light Brigade' received an irreparable dent. It now hangs in the dining room with its companions.

We were married on the 20 July 1957 and I have never ceased to thank God for giving me a second chance. Jimmy was the dearest and best of husbands. He was completely unselfish and always loving and protective. I know he trusted and believed in me and his encouragement gave me confidence in myself. We may have been very short of money at times, but we were always happy. Jimmy was always responsible in planning for my security if I was left without him. He was a tremendous worker and put his heart into anything he undertook, so I always felt I was running to keep up with him. But we tackled everything as a team and that made everything fun.

Having recently attended a wedding that had everything except a military band, I was determined that ours should be very simple.

1957 Our Wedding
From left to right: Jimmy's father Ronald Robertson; Bill Stamford;
My Mother Tina O'Carroll Scott; Jimmy & self; Jimmy's Mother Molly
Robertson; my Father Tony O'Carroll Scott; Margaret Ralston.

D had offered me a London wedding, but I much preferred to be married in the little church in the village that I knew so well amongst the people I had grown up with. So we had no morning coats and no carnation buttonholes, just lounge suits and rose buttonholes. I was twenty-nine and I thought I was far too old to be married in white with little bridesmaids. And so my full-skirted three quarter length dress was pale primrose. Two friends from Constance Spry decorated the church with roses and the reception was held in the village hall. My mother had raised a fatigue party to help her clean the hut beforehand, and in the process they discovered a hitherto unknown drain. They also uncovered what they imagined to be a mouse hole in the church but this turned out to be an entry to a family vault.

Jimmy took me to France for our honeymoon and we set off in Nunky's beautiful old drop head Rover. He had lent my parents his current car for their honeymoon thirty-one years before. We spent two nights in Paris at a luxurious hotel, which had flowers in our room and endless cupboards and after that we made our way south through Chartres to the Tarn Province where we stayed in an idyllically pretty medieval town called Cordes sur Ciel, which stood on a hill surrounded by vineyards. We returned home through Brittany and Normandy, looking at chateaux and battlefields, having collected various pieces of French silver and china in little out of the way antique shops. Everything had gone smoothly until our last day when we had two burst tyres. We were towed backwards into Calais and the AA had two new tyres waiting for us at Dover. All this took some time and at 1:00 a.m. Jimmy was faced with having to drive to East Sussex. I asked the mechanic if he knew of an overnight café who could give us some coffee. He replied, 'No, there's nothing open now but you can come home with me, my wife will get you something.' The dear woman came downstairs in her curlers and gave us coffee and sandwiches and I only wish I had kept a record of their address to write and thank her again, but I shall never forget their kindness.

We thought our first home would be Shoeburyness but soon after our return from our honeymoon Jimmy learned that he was to be appointed to the Regular Commissions Board in Westbury. Jimmy had always loved Salisbury Plain and wished he could take me there and this was a perfect posting, for he would be working intensely mid-week and then have a long weekend off. The candidates for the Regular Commissions Board were given various nearly impossible tasks to complete with their teams. They were judged not so much on completing their tasks – it could be the crossing of a crocodile infested river with one rope and a plank which would not reach the far shore, – but to prove how capable they were when leading their teams in considerable stress. The WRACs had to undertake similar tasks. Thankfully, future wives were not given such problems to solve.

Our first home was an army quarter in a quiet, secluded road and we probably gave our neighbours much to think about when we agreed to walk two hound puppies for the RA Hunt. Jimmy had walked Daystar the reserve champion dog hound at Peterborough in 1954, so he knew all about hound puppies but this was a new experience for me. Jimmy had built them a spacious kennel and a run made out of a redundant hut for RCB candidates. Unfortunately, the gate opened outwards and when I took out their feeding bowls both puppies jumped up at the gate, which swung back onto my eye. When you have only recently been married, having to face your neighbours looking like a giant panda can be rather embarrassing. Jimmy would take the two puppies and our black Labrador, Tern, for a run every day to say good morning to Westbury's white horse.

And now I have a story with a moral. If kindly friends suggest that you keep the top layer of your wedding cake to use for the Christening cake, don't take any notice; just eat it! We dutifully kept the top of our cake in a sealed up tin and asked the delightful old-fashioned grocer in Warminster to keep it for us amongst their homemade jams and pickles. We had dearly longed for our own family and being twenty-nine I hoped it would arrive soon. But our prayers were not answered. My parents could not have been more tactful, I know they would have been thrilled with having grandchildren but they never referred to it. Neither did Jimmy's father and uncle, the dearest, kindest of men. But Jimmy's mother was not so restrained and she gave me a positive guilt complex because she insinuated it was all my fault.

Poor Mum, she was beautiful and gracious and could be a lovely companion, but the fairies at her Christening had left out the gifts of personal relationships and a sense of humour. She was one of those sad people who were born with an unhappy, 'I feel so sorry for myself' trait in her personality. She had married a loving, generous war hero who had been a top class games player before the First World War, playing cricket for Middlesex and rugger for Scotland. He had served in the Gordon Highlanders in the First World War and lost an eye and a leg but he was incredibly brave and never complained. I think Mum imagined she would have been blissful with a classical scholar who had lofty thoughts about music and ancient Greece.

Dad could never be rude or angry to any woman but he could avenge his frustration on poor blameless Nunky and the result was quite a lot of tension in what should have been a happy house. Apart from Jimmy's mother, I had a certain amount of hopeful pressure from the kindly grocer. 'Would I be wanting the cake?' they asked with curious shining eyes. In the end, I decided the best solution was to eat it for Easter. In the meantime, Jimmy and I consoled ourselves by thinking how disastrous it would have been if our child had inherited all the more trying characteristics of some of the family. Another Aunt Doris did not bear thinking about.

CHAPTER TEN

House Hunting

Very soon after our move to Westbury, we began house hunting. We both had a strong nesting instinct and we opened a file LOP (lovely old place). Jimmy's Aunt Elsie had been married to Sir William Arrol, the builder of the Forth Bridge and when she died, she left him a generous legacy. As I was far away at the time, he had no long-term plans for his future and he spent part of it on hunting and polo. But when we became engaged there was still enough left to spend on a cottage. Jimmy tackled this scientifically and he drew a fifteen-mile radius round Lark Hill where he hoped he might be posted. We searched the Salisbury area with no success. We looked at cottages with mushrooms growing out of the ceiling and houses that had been partially destroyed by fire and there was one mystery cottage, which had disappeared into the mist like Brigadoon for we never found it again.

Finally, Jimmy said, 'I think we must look around the Andover area.' You may remember that geography was not my best subject and I had never heard of Andover. But we set out for the house agents and I remember quite clearly picking up a leaflet which advertised a thatched cottage with a workshop of 26 ft. and my first reaction was, 'Well that will keep him quiet,' because I had already witnessed a dog kennel being built in the dining room of our army quarter. I don't think we realised how lucky we were at the time.

Penton Mewsey was a quiet village, not so quiet now as it was in the 50s, but the road, which passed our garden gate, was a back road to Newbury and the front of the cottage faced inwards, south towards the garden. In the 18th century it had been the Bell Inn and in Victorian times it was a wheelwright and beer house. Although it had made a very pleasant home for an elderly lady, there was a lot to be done and we had a year to do it before Jimmy received another posting. Rose Cottage had been built of brick and flint into the side of a fairly steep hill, for the village street followed the line of what had been a river in Roman times. Luckily we were above flood level in the winter but we had the problem of how to get up and down to the top garden in the easiest possible way.

Jimmy and D put their heads together and they decided to take away several tons of earth from the steep bank and replace it with a zigzag path up the sheer face. The side of the hill would be planted with Clematis and Virginia Creeper when it had been faced with brick and cement. It made a charming background to a crazy paved courtyard with a pond. When the bulldozer arrived to take away the soil, we found that the steep bank had been the village rubbish dump and they uncovered medieval pottery from the lowest layer, a ship's decanter and an 18th century wine bottle a little higher up topped up with a German helmet and a shell. When I was told about the shell, my first reaction was, what a long way from the sea, but it turned out to be a- very-much-alive shell, which had probably been picked up on one of the nearby ranges. It was taken away with great solemnity by a bomb disposal team and a policeman and blown up.

Meanwhile, D was walking round the garden having the time of his life. 'James, you don't want that tree there,' he would exclaim. Altogether, he condemned seven trees but it was a great improvement and we were able to plant something far prettier. Jimmy has always believed in firm foundations, I tend to start by planning curtains and the more exciting things but he was determined to concentrate on making the cottage warm and draught proof. So, he insulated the ceilings and dug down a good two feet under the drawing room floor so that there would be an air space for the new floorboards. With the help of the village cricket tean, who we nicknamed 'the Midnight

Builders', we knocked down walls and blocked up certain door-ways. We turned the carpenter's workshop into a delightful dining room, we opened the back of the baker's oven into the drawing room showing a deep cave and a brick arch over another vaulted cavity, which must have been designed to hold a barrel. The drawing room fire had burned well but Jimmy had pulled the whole thing out to reveal a large cavity, which was ideal for a wood-burning stove.

In order to save money, Jimmy put in a bath and various basins himself and the plumber came along to link everything up. But to add to the work, Jimmy decided to build on a larger bedroom for ourselves, which would catch the morning sun and underneath I would have my own study or burrow. This extension to the cottage must have seemed an unnecessary extravagance for people with no children but Jimmy's idea was to cut the cottage in two when he was posted abroad, so that we could claim the rent from two army hirings. We had paid for the cottage but the various improvements had run up a small overdraft.

Throughout his life, Jimmy refused to owe anyone money except the bank and although we got on extremely well with the bank, the manager had been rather agitated at the thought of us running up an overdraft of about two thousand pounds. I was quite reasonably virtuous and when the family offered me luxury items for my birthday I said, 'What we really want is screws.' But Jimmy was proved right over the years, for when D died, we were able to move my mother straight into her own set of rooms when she came to live with us. The cottage has always had a happy welcoming feeling even when it was under partial dismantlement and I was glad to see the old beams and part of the natural brickwork in the kitchen and the drawing room. Apart from being attractive, they reminded me of our foundations and roots and we felt in sympathy with those who built and worked in the cottage years before.

We might not have a Christening but I wanted the house we loved so much to have God's blessing and in the midst of piles of timber and paint pots we invited an old army friend of Jimmy's who had taken orders to come over with his wife and little boy to give us a short service of blessing. The only other person present was darling Auntie Mamie, and Ronald made it a very special service. Our dining room was a little unusual in that some fifty years before, an aeroplane had been built there. It never flew, because it was powered by a motorbike engine, but it had been tenderly carried up to the racecourse where it taxied quietly into a hedge. The builders had been the Squire's son and the village carpenter.

Rose Cottage and the Midnight Builders.

CHAPTER ELEVEN

A Fairy House

~~~~~~

In 1960, Jimmy learned that he was to be posted to Cyprus and, as the posting was only for five months, I was lucky to be allowed to go with him, and after all Jimmy's work and planning we were able to divide the cottage in two. We let both sides of the cottage. In the midst of our house hunting, we had hired some horses from the stables at Larkhill so that we might hack over Salisbury Plain, but sadly it turned out to be impossible. While I was in Australia I had fallen over a chair and nearly broken my pelvis and sitting in the saddle turned out to be agony. On one occasion Jimmy had to abandon me with Tern our black Labrador, take the horses back to the stables and collect us in ourA35 van. Jimmy was unselfish, he never grumbled or blamed me; he just said he didn't want to ride without me and as it turned out there would have been no time for riding once we started work on the cottage.

We arrived in Cyprus in January and rented a small modern, bitterly cold bungalow. One imagines Cyprus to be always warm, but in the winter months, one needs something more than two oil stoves. Jimmy had been given command of his own Battery, VIII Alma Battery and, anticipating the battery celebration for Alma Day and being a military historian, he decided to dress up his men in uniforms of the period. It was up to us wives to make up the costumes and we squashed all pretensions of rank consciousness by making a gunner's wife the cutter. I became intimately aware of the condition of some of the men's feet and even underwear, but it was all great fun. There was one tense moment when the battery Sergeant-Major forgot to collect Bombardier Hatch's wife for the group photograph. When the transport eventually appeared, her mouth was set in a furious line and she refused to join in. I remember saying, 'Oh please Mrs. Hatch, do come just for me, it wouldn't be complete without you.' The old photograph shows the smiling group including Mrs. Hatch and myself with our arms practically around each other's necks.

Jimmy had bought a second-hand Fiat for our time in Cyprus. I still wonder how he managed to get into it. At weekends we drove all over that beautiful island, which was recovering from one set of troubles but had not yet been divided into two parts for the Turks and the Greeks. There were some incredible archaeological sites and living in Famagusta on the east side of the island, we were able to see some of the excavations on Salamis the ancient city, which had welcomed St. Paul before it was buried by an earthquake and a tidal wave.

When we returned home, Jimmy was posted to the Citadel in Plymouth with his battery. We had not wanted to go into an army quarter, preferring to be independent. While we were engaged, I had seen how some army quarters become open houses and one does not always want to encounter one's next-door neighbour in the bathroom. We put our names down with a house agent and, although we returned home to no fixed address, on our very first day in Plymouth we discovered that there was a small one storey Georgian house to be rented on the Earl of Mount Edgcumbe's estate, just across Plymouth Sound. The Garden House was a fairy house, rather like the *Petit Trianon* in the park of Versailles. It stood in four acres of cultivated garden set in the main park. There was the Italian garden with its orangery, graceful stairway and ornamental pool; the French garden, a little sad and shadowy except for a beautiful urn, which was dedicated:

> *To her, whose grace embellished, whose presence*
> *added charms to these retreats. Herself their brightest*
> *ornament. This urn is erected in a place she loved.*

I do not know who 'she' was.

Our little house had been built in the 18th century in the English garden. There was a portico over the Egyptian doorway, which led into the dining room cum hall. On one side was our bedroom with its original bamboo wallpaper and, on the other, a tiny drawing room with an alcove draped with muslin curtains that contained a small sofa. For some time, we had been gradually collecting our own furniture. Apart from raiding family lofts, we had hunted through every second hand shop and junk shop in sight. Jimmy would allow me one shop per long journey and we found some astonishing bargains. It was before *The Antiques Road Show* caught people's imagination. Our dining room table had been made for us by a little cabinetmaker in Norfolk, so our furniture, though not valuable, fitted in with the little house. We looked out onto a lovely lawn, which was surrounded by every shade of rhododendron and azalea. The first magnolia to be brought into England grew outside the drawing room window and there were cork trees, a handkerchief tree, and other rare and beautiful shrubs. On moon lit nights the deer sometimes jumped over the wall from the park and galloped across the lawn.

1962. Mt Edgcumbe - The Garden House

Jimmy used to park the car at the marine barracks in Plymouth and in the mornings he would run down the garden path to the Cremyll Ferry for the five-minute crossing. Mount Edgcumbe Castle had been bombed during the war and while we were there, the restoration was completed. Lord and Lady Mount Edgcumbe were a loveable elderly couple and they were wonderfully kind to us, including us in many of their parties. One night while we slept, a huge ilex tree growing just behind the house fell down, bringing with it the drawing room chimney, the electricity cable and the telephone, as well as uprooting the water main. I was preparing for the worst with pints of milk and packets of candles when Lord Mount Edgcumbe who was well into his eighties arrived with his foresters and by midday we were reconnected all round.

If we walked down a garden path, twisting through a twenty foot ilex hedge, we came onto the battery with its captured French guns and we felt we could reach out and touch the Ark Royal when she slipped past under the battery wall and of course there had to be a ghost. Sometime in the 18th century one of the former Lords of Mount Edgcumbe used to spend much of his time in the Garden House. There he would read and write and escape from the world and he was always accompanied by his beloved dog. I believe it was a very big dog, something like a wolfhound. The years passed and the old dog died but the Earl was so lost without his dear companion that he had him stuffed and hung up in the little house.

During the war, the Americans were camped in the park waiting for D Day. When they saw the old dog they decided he was looking very shabby and rather moth eaten and so they buried him with due ceremony on the edge of the lawn, which was kept as a dog cemetery for the Castle pets. After the war ended Mr. Edward Edgcumbe and his wife Effie made their home in the garden house and Effie was disturbed and a little puzzled when she became aware of being followed by a dog when she walked through the grounds. She could see nothing but she could hear him panting and she could also hear him scratching on the glass door in the hall, which led into the garden. Jimmy certainly heard him and Tern was definitely aware of him, because all his back hair came up and he would growl and bark at a seemingly empty lawn. I found it rather unnerving when I was alone in the house while Jimmy was dining out at a mess night and so I would open the door, tell Tern firmly that this other dog had lived here long before he did and they would just have to share the house together. But Auntie Mamie actually felt him for she was sleeping in the room where he had been kept for so many years and she told me that a dog had nuzzled her with his nose during the night. I knew it could not be Tern because I had blocked her door with a chair.

It was wonderful to live in such idyllic surroundings and we knew we were incredibly lucky. When Alma Day came round again we had a big buffet lunch on the lawn for all Jimmy's officers and warrant officers and their wives. We also invited Jimmy's Colonel and his wife and his fellow officers from the Regiment. There had been a big church parade at the Citadel in the morning and then Jimmy brought all the guests over by launch, where they were entertained by their RA band on the lawn. It may have been fun but I'm sure it ruined Jimmy's promotion. Jimmy was an individualist, a 'one-off', as some of his friends described him. He was a military historian and he loved putting on a pageant or a play. He was a most generous host and he enjoyed seizing opportunities to celebrate, not from any sense of self-glorification but to give pleasure to friends.

When he had marched his whole battery from Larkhill to Okehampton in five days carrying all their equipment, Jimmy himself carried the heaviest piece, the base plate. On reaching Okehampton they had celebrated by firing their guns. His fellow Battery Commanders thought he was mad, but many years later our soldiers carried out a similar feat in the Falklands when the *Sir Galahad* was sunk. He had also taken the entire battery up to Olympia to see the

Royal Tournament but one of his contemporaries remarked, 'I wish I had thought of that first.' I'm afraid Jimmy's Colonel and some of his fellow officers were resentful. We had been marked down because we did not want to live in an army quarter and I had already been called 'toffee nosed' because I had chosen to have breakfast in my hotel bedroom before we embarked for home, rather than face a noisy dining room. And for this grievous sin some of the wives sent me to Coventry on our journey home. I was surprised and rather amused when one of these wives knocked on my cabin door just before we landed to ask if I would give her a new pair of tights.

This was all very childish, but Jimmy's Colonel did not follow up his previous excellent confidential report, which had strongly recommended him to have his own Regiment. I have to be honest and admit this may have been partly Jimmy's own fault. He did not respect the Colonel and showed it. Nothing would have made him say, 'Oh Colonel, you're wonderful,' if he didn't think it and politically it would have paid him to be a perfect hypocrite. But sometimes a setback or disappointment can turn out for the best. It resulted in Jimmy deciding to retire from the Army two years later and take up teaching and for twenty years he was able to put all his energy and concern into caring for children.

CHAPTER TWELVE

Hectic Years

Jimmy decided he was going to have a proper certificate behind him and go in for teaching in a state school, rather than find a comfy lily pond in some prep school. And as it happened there was a teacher's training college about fifteen miles away from the cottage for mature students on a two-year course. But it was going to be a very tight squeeze existing for two years on his army pension, without running up another overdraft. Then Jimmy read the small print. This declared that if a mature student were married to another mature student he or she would qualify for a grant. I used to tease him years later and said, 'You know you never asked me darling, you just said well you can come with me.'

The thought of teaching horrified me, but I thought well if I stick to Brownie age perhaps, it won't be so bad. Some years before when we were working on the cottage, I had been made a District Commissioner for Guides. The only reason for this was that the County Commissioner who lived in the village was desperate and couldn't find anyone else. The uniform was a slight compensation and I was proud of my hat with its blue cockade but I was terrified that I would be faced with a situation, which called for knowledge, initiative, and authority. I had been a rotten guide myself and I suspect that my patrol leader had gone on to be a leading light in a women's prison, but England expected and I must just try and do my best.

One thing I could do was to cheer on the guiders who were doing all the work and thank them. My worst moment came when one of the guiders invited their Commissioner to come and inspect the Brownies and see their knots. By now I knew the difference between a reef and a granny and I set out for a neighbouring village not forgetting to take my packet of pepper in case I met some menacing stranger on the dark walk home. To my consternation I was welcomed, not only by the Brownies, but by a hall full of eager parents all waiting for the dear Commissioner to speak. I dare not imagine what nonsense I came out with, but I gave them two recommendations for the future. Always know what your object is and give yourself time to think every day.

We began our two-year course at the teacher's training college full of hope and high expectation. Sadly, it turned out to be a time of considerable frustration. Half the trouble was that the teaching staff had no idea how to deal with mature students. We had all had considerable experience of life in various careers but, instead of harnessing any talents we might have had, they overcame their own inferiority complex by attempting to demoralise and intimidate us. There was a legend that a retired Admiral who had gone through the course sometime before us, cornered the history teacher behind her desk and exploded, 'Don't you dare speak to me like that!' And the geography tutor who had produced khaki twins was chased round

1964. Teachers training...

her room by an irate retired Major. So, this may explain why they had turned down the application of a retired naval Commander who had been recommended for a VC, because they explained his maths was not up to the course.

But it was all rather exasperating being treated like backward infants when we had the terrible prospect of failure hanging over us. Some of the tutors had a strong left-wing bias like so many of the current textbooks and they resented anyone who did not share their own background. But of course, there are always exceptions and we became very fond of certain individuals. One was Dr. Roy Rich, professor of philosophy who took some of our lectures on education. He was delighted to discover that he had worked with great Uncle James when he was Vice Chancellor of Leeds University. Great Uncle James had married Auntie Lena, one of Grandpa's sisters who could have been the model for Lady Bracknell. Although undoubtedly kind and generous, she could be formidable. Who else could attend a cricket match at Lords and poke one of the fielders in the back saying, 'Sit down young man, I can't see!' And Dr. Rich recounted an occasion when he had been staying at some university house party and Auntie Lena appeared on an upper landing exclaiming in distracted tones, 'Sir James has never slept in the room in which he has undressed.'

Dr. Rich wanted me to do a study of Plato for my extended study but I lost my nerve, thinking I would be behind with my reading and I chose current problems in education instead. I could do this at the kitchen table and unleash all my anger in lofty thoughts on mucky blah. I must say that the greatest benefit we achieved from our tedious books on sociology was to sell the lot and go out for an excellent dinner at the end of our course on the proceeds.

It has always surprised me that service men and women have to be positively vetted and put through gruelling testing before they are given a commission. But in our day, almost anybody could become a teacher. All that was needed was two recommendations from kindly friends and in my case an indifferent school certificate. When I had my first interview with the Deputy Principal, I noticed an endearing photograph of a fox terrier on her desk and I admired it. Her eyes lit up and from then on the entire interview seemed to be about dogs. Dogs we had owned, dogs that we liked, the training of dogs. It was all very enjoyable and it was the beginning of a firm friendship because she was a dear, but she never asked me if I liked children and why I wanted to take up teaching. Rumour had it that she had once been a sharp shooter in a circus and she was certainly a loveable eccentric. We had wondered why she had never returned our essays and we then discovered that what she thought to be a cupboard in a flat in the Cathedral close was really a fire escape.

Jimmy sensibly opted to take history and here he was lucky to be taught by Barry Shipley, a keen archaeologist and the very best kind of old-fashioned schoolmaster. He had an equally loveable wife and I used to tie myself on to the various history outings when I could. Jimmy had been set to work making an elephant out of a ragbag when the Principal came to inspect that department. 'Now Major Robertson what do you think of this course?' he inquired. 'Do you really want to know?' replied Jimmy and the poor man fled.

The sixties were noted for being permissive and what went on in the junior common room was sometimes startling to say the least. Jimmy and I were amused when some student enquired about us. Is that large man courting that lady? I could face most things when Jimmy was there but when he was about his own affairs I homed on to two large, very kindly petty officers. The most depressing part of the course was that we were never taught how to teach. Fortunately, Jimmy knew so he could help me. I was never taught how to teach children to read, although I was aiming to teach juniors and there were no lessons in first aid, something that is a daily necessity in a primary school. And if the outside world was going quietly dotty in the sixties the educationists were having a field day. Self-expression was the 'in' thing and formal maths, tables, grammar, discipline, and duty were out of date.

Fortunately, once I had my own class I discovered that I could have brainwashed children with Chairman Mao's little red book once the classroom door was closed. Instead we quietly got on with spelling and learning our tables and I tried to teach the children to be pleasant, thoughtful people. At College, I was told it was no good taking history and English or RI because as a married woman I would not have time to read. Instead, I was pushed into taking art and craft. The needlework mistress had a hate on married women and she was so rude the first time I met her that I knew I could not be happy in her department, it would be impossible. The creative art tutor tried to get us students to get him pornographic books so that was obviously impossible. The sculpture department spent their time making scrap metal objects which had a nightmarish impact on me, but their creators imagined them to be in tune with their emotions and were positively visionary having great depth, structure and texture in the language of Jabberwocky:

> *'Twas brillig, and the slithy toves*
> *Did gyre and gimble in the wabe,*
> *All mimsy were the borogoves*
> *And the mome raths outgrabe.*

All that was left to me was pottery. As a child I never enjoyed making mud pies but it had to be faced. I knew I had to put on a display at the end of the course and rather than leave everything to the last month I decided to produce one thing per week or fortnight. I was afraid that if I tried the wheel, I would end up with a row of lopsided cups and bowls. So I opted to do coil and slab and if they wanted something odd they should have it. So, my display was based on various fruits and berries. Much against my will, I almost started to enjoy pottery, especially when I enrolled in the local further education class in Andover. Here there was a very kind, competent tutor who believed in running a well-organised, clean pottery room but I never taught pottery to my children. They might well have enjoyed it, but it can be rather like chalk carving, tricky in the classroom and it's more important to keep the caretaker.

Although we had Jimmy's army pension and my grant, surviving for two years with no other money coming in was going to be rather a struggle. Admittedly we could now meet our bank manager with clear conscience, but we cut down on everything, even a second cup of coffee. Just occasionally we had a treat and the very sympathetic owner of a small thatched pub nearby gave us dinner for two. It was the same as he and his family were having and he changed us a pound. Then Jimmy discovered that if we put our names down to take part in road censuses during the holidays, we could earn a little extra pocket money. Our first census was on a boiling hot bank holiday on one of the main roads leading into Southampton. There were eight of us but the only thing which might have prevented the steaming motorists from exploding as they were stopped and asked their destination, was the front row of the chorus of the Windmill Theatre.

I was flattered to be given one sweet and the offer of a lift, but it was quite intimidating having huge vehicles practically touching us as they passed us. Jimmy told me that at the end of our eight hour stint I asked him, 'Darling what is an articulated vehicle?' and after he told me I had replied, 'Oh I put them all down as articulated vehicles!' I didn't believe him, but it so happens that that road has about six lanes so perhaps I made someone happy.

We took part in four censuses and earned forty pounds, Jimmy being given a pound more than me because he was in charge. Our best day was when we were put in a very sleepy side road at the bottom of an old lady's garden with one really nice Police Constable. The old lady insisted on bringing us pots of tea on a silver tray and our police friend remarked, 'You could do this with your eyes shut.' If you hear pant, pant, pant you know there is a bicycle going up hill and if you hear tick, tick, tick you know there is a bicycle freewheeling downhill.

Although I had originally planned to forget about teaching, once we left college with our certificates, that year 1966, I found myself starting a new life and a new career. It was to last for the next twenty years. We were very fortunate in finding jobs not too far from our cottage, so we did not have to face hours spent commuting. Jimmy's first job was in a small comprehensive school about thirteen miles away and every morning he would drop me off at my Church of England primary school, which was about four miles from home. The school had only just been opened. There were two classrooms, one for the infants and one for the senior children. I would be teaching the seven to nines in the hall. Everything was shining new and gleaming with paint but I have to be honest, it was difficult to make an intimate base with the children. Teaching in the hall was rather like teaching on Waterloo Station, although a low screen divided us from the coats and basins of the cloakroom. But when the doctor or dentist called, I felt I was also trying to indoctrinate the row of invisible mothers who were chattering away the other side of the partition.

The children had so-called 'family friendly' tables and a drawer to keep their work in. These tables being hexagonal may have been useful for lunch and art and craft, but they made it impossible for all the children to see the blackboard and encouraged chatter when they should have been concentrating on the work. Nevertheless, I was proud to have my very own class and I felt a bit like a mother duck gathering her young about her.

At some time or other we all have to face a really embarrassing moment in our lives and mine came fairly soon after I started teaching at Appleshaw. Being a new school and very up-to-date, we actually had two cloakrooms; one for the headmaster who did not need to share it with anyone except a visiting HMI and one for all the female teachers and kitchen staff. It was all very clinical and hanging on the wall was a chromium box for burning things only needed in the ladies cloakroom. Nobody touched the thing until one day I decided it would be very convenient and I turned it on and returned to the classroom. I cannot remember how long it was before someone discovered that smoke was pouring out of the cloakroom and filtering into the classroom and the kitchen. We carried out our fire drill and the school was evacuated onto the playground. Our headmaster found it very hard to explain the reason for the fire to the children. He decided the need to burn important confidential papers was the best explanation. Fortunately nothing else was involved, but we later discovered that the architect who had installed this useful gadget had forgotten to include a chimney.

I spent four years at Appleshaw and the only dramatic moment came at the time of one of the first teacher strikes. Jimmy and I were firmly resolved never to strike when it would affect the children. To Jimmy it would have been tantamount to mutiny, so when the headmaster ordered the school to close, I continued working in my classroom. The building was fairly isolated and when I answered the telephone a sinister voice growled out down the receiver, 'black leg.' Normally the primary schools were not so militant, but Jimmy in his comprehensive school had a wretched time, being abused verbally and physically by some of his colleagues after he refused to take part in any strike. He once received a solicitor's letter sent to him by a Master in the next classroom. That same master liked to play *The Red Flag* really loudly so Jimmy retaliated with *Rule Britannia*.

I have always been fond of children and those in my class became my substitute family, even though they sometimes sent me quite demented. Seven to nine is a delightful age to teach. You don't have to concentrate on toilet training, although there was one small boy who I always released from the class when he approached me with pleading, untruthful eyes. 'It's paper Miss, urgent.' It wasn't worth the risk. But it is still an age of comparative innocence and they are always keen to learn and fascinated by stories and legends. I realised however that I had to learn a new language to link in with their very simple, basic way of thinking. One sultry afternoon I was attempting to teach the children what we all need in order to survive. Eventually, after a great effort they admitted that we did need light, heat and food. 'Now come along,' I said brightly, 'I'm sure you can think of something else, which we simply must have.' Vicky, a doctor's daughter was sitting at the back of the class. She had been sent up to Class II a year early because she was so bright. Her classmates were quietly nodding in the heat but she looked at me seriously and put up her hand. 'Watercress,' she suggested. It was many months afterwards that I discovered that her mother adored watercress. It was Vicky who asked me the question that I have never been able to answer.

'Mrs. Robertson,' she inquired, 'What is civilisation?' Normally if I was stuck I would reply that I would look it up or ask my husband, but this one was a snorter. Does it mean law and order? But that could include horrendous tortures and imprisonment. Does it mean beauty? But how much beauty has been achieved with slave labour. Does it mean good drainage? I still find it hard to answer. I'm sure cleanliness, compassion and mercy must be included somewhere but it is a puzzle. When Vicky grew up and left school we gave her a copy of Kenneth Clarke's *Civilisation*. He certainly gave us many answers but perhaps not all.

On another occasion, I was trying to explain the role of part-time firemen. 'So you see, children, when the fire bell goes, all the part-time firemen drop whatever they are doing and rush off to the fire.' Kevin was a delightful child with large eyes and long eyelashes. Like his sister, clean clothes usually meant an extra layer on top of the other. His father worked in the local slaughterhouse and at weekends,

Kevin helped him in the muck room. He looked at me very seriously. 'What happens if it is breakable Miss?' he inquired. But sometimes I felt deeply humbled by their clear insight and understanding. We were in the midst of the Easter story, a story, which can be very painful to tell and I asked the children what they thought St. Peter must have felt when he had said three times that he did not know his best friend and Jesus turned and looked at him. 'Untough,' replied Trevor whose previous school had been a very tough one in Glasgow and who, I strongly suspected, now slept on the floor of his home with few blankets.

In this life, our knowledge of truth and wisdom must inevitably be limited. I have sometimes envisaged the glory of God, which contains all knowledge, all wisdom. It is like a burning fiery furnace covered with a metal screen. Some of us will never know the wonder that is hidden by the screen. It will always remain a mystery but some, a few with eyes to see and minds to understand, are permitted to see through a tiny chink in that cover and sometimes, just sometimes young children can see more clearly than their elders.

I was happy at Appleshaw but whatever I did to my classroom, it always seemed as if it was like a dentist's surgery, and every day we lost a good ten minutes when all our tables were moved for lunch. After four years, two vacancies appeared. One was in a small exclusive private school and one was in the Church of England school about a mile and a half from our cottage. I can't imagine why I agreed to be interviewed by the private school. The headmistress was elderly and charming and the children looked to be delightful. But a games mistress! I must have been mad. Not all the bluff in the world would have disguised the fact that I could not see a ball let alone hit it. So when I was offered the post I politely declined and accepted the position of teacher to Class II at Weyhill Church of England Primary School, which became my second home for the next nine years.

My classroom and the infant's classroom were based in a so-called temporary classroom behind the old Victorian school. The children sat in old-fashioned desks facing the blackboard and outside one of the windows a chaffinch had built its nest in an old lichen-covered apple tree. Here at last I had a classroom door, which I could close and we could become a small family in a room decorated with pictures and displays and maps. The room may have been old and battered but to me it was heaven and I would like to think the children were happy too.

There was one hectic moment when I was on my knees in the book corner playing a reading game with some of the slow learners, when I became aware that the heavy bookcase standing against the wall was not only leaning ominously towards us but was slowly sinking through the floor. Fortunately, we all evacuated the mat in time. I once saw the disadvantage of every child having his own desk. On the day, we were preparing the classroom for the parents to come to see their children's work that evening, everything was looking tidy and clean, and I could not think why Christopher should be nervous of his mother seeing his work. She was a sweet soul and his work had been excellent that term but just as we were admiring our handy work and preparing to go home for tea Christopher opened up his desk again and was very, very sick.

Whenever I recall my time in Class II, I think of William. One evening I received a tearful telephone call from Antonia, the youngest daughter of the owner of the manor house, which stands opposite our cottage. I knew she was newly married to Maurice, a young pilot. 'Oh June, you must help me, Maurice says he can't have him leaving yellow hair all over his blue uniform and if he doesn't go, he will and Mummy says she'll only keep him for a week.' It appeared that Antonia, who had a very loving heart, had found William, a large rather gangly yellow Labrador puppy, tied up to a kennel with a chain strong enough to hold a fully grown lion. She had bought him for a pound and taken him home, but as he was in full puppy moult, his reception was limited. Jimmy faced with two tearful women, came up with sound common sense. 'We will have him,' he said, 'if your headmistress allows me to build a run for him outside your classroom.

Miss B was a strange, very private, person. She had undoubted talents in art and music but I found it hard to understand her and often felt she resented me. There was one subject on which we could agree. She liked dogs and had two Yorkshire Terriers of her own. When Jimmy asked her if she would allow William to have his own establishment, she said, 'I don't see why not.' Jimmy started at dawn the next day and erected the hound puppy's kennel and the faithful wire enclosure, which had been restored, together with a platform of railway sleepers so William would not have to sit out in the mud. An old plum tree gave partial shade to the run and it stood against the school fence well above the pond, which tended to flood in winter.

I was glad Miss B. was away from school the first day that William joined Class II. It was a very wet afternoon and the ridiculous puppy was sitting out in the rain ignoring his lovely kennel packed with straw. I set Class II, six lines of copy writing and I put on my Macintosh, sou'wester and gumboots. I then proceeded to half coax; half push a reluctant puppy into the straw. I returned to Class II but we were interrupted. 'Please Miss, he's out again.' It took a little time for everyone to settle down but William proved to be a definite success. They could love him and talk to him through the wire and they were very distressed to learn about his unhappy puppyhood. He became our mascot and teaching aid. Punctuation lessons were based on William. William (capital letter) is going to have a birthday soon. Are you coming to his party (question mark). Oh dear, William has eaten my slipper (exclamation mark)! Etc. etc.

William did have a birthday party. It started in a modest way with the children acting the story of St. Swithin outside his kennel run,

About 1970 - William joins Class II.

then it grew to be a major event. Every year we would persuade about a half a dozen selfless grownups to fill their cars with children and we would take them round Winchester Cathedral. I had been telling them stories about the Cathedral all the term. We would then return to the cottage and have a birthday tea with a large cake made in the shape of a Labrador's head with smarties around the collar telling us William's age. This would be made by my very dear Cinders who has been a much loved friend and has helped me to look after the cottage for over thirty years. The selfless grownups once included a bishop but it was all great fun and William would sit among his pile of presents well aware that they were all for him.

The back of our small, rather dilapidated school looked over the village pond. On the other side we could see the occasional deer gallop across the ploughed field from a small wooded copse; the rooks fussed about their nursery in the tall beech tree on the other side of the road. There was no effort to keep a diary of the farming year and a chart of the seasons. We made great friends with Willie Scambler, a very wise, elderly farmer who rented much of the land surrounding the school. And he showed us round his young calves and asked the children to play in his cornfield. We also went for nature walks through the wood owned by the Forestry Commission.

These were happy days but I sometimes wondered how the children absorbed any formal lessons at all. Apart from visits from the doctor and the dentist and the library, the register and the dinner money always seemed to cut into the timetable. And there were always interruptions for lost property. No child ever seemed to remember what clothes he or she came to school in and if you held out a pair of shoes or a jumper, you would be greeted with blank faces. Added to which, there were always interruptions from a passing wasp or a loose tooth and other problems of more serious nature. Besides losing their teeth in class, many children lost their grandparents and I would have found this very hard to deal with if I had not been convinced that our Lord was always there tucked into a corner, waiting to be appealed to. For without his teaching and his love for us nothing would have made sense. After all, why shouldn't we all lie, steal, cheat, and bully our neighbour? One small child who had not been told about the love of God really imagined her granny would be taken to the dump when she was worn out.

In spite of all my corkscrew justice in a sea of red herrings, it was sometimes desperately hard not to laugh. One day I was confronted by three angelic-looking small boys in my class and it was obviously serious stuff. It appeared that Tony and Andrew had been calling Roy 'Chocolate Drop' because his skin was a milky coffee shade. Roy was sensitive about his colour and had paid the other two boys two pence a go not to call him names. They appeared to think this was fair, but the trouble became complicated when it appeared that the two pence had been taken out of Roy's mother's electric meter and she could not understand how much more electricity they were using. After giving the two blackmailers an imperial rocket, I turned to Roy and told him he had been very silly to make such a fuss about his colour.

'But I'm black,' he cried in great distress. 'Nonsense,' I replied. 'Your skin is just like Jesus and it is a very pretty colour.'

I suppose it is inevitable that some of the children's funnier remarks should have come in scripture lessons. Apparently when the disciples had been urged by our Lord to cast their nets on the other side of the boat after a frustratingly blank night's fishing, St Peter was heard to say, 'Well what have we got to lose?' But I think the best account came from Jean, who was a perpetual problem. Her conscience was stunted if not totally undeveloped and she was always helping herself to my lozenges.

'Jean!' I exclaimed after finding her with her hand in the box, 'How can you enjoy eating something which does not belong to you?'

'Oh but I do,' she replied, 'They are delicious.' However when she came to describe our Lord's meeting with Mary Magdalene in the garden after the resurrection, she wrote that Jesus had said, 'I am rose but don't touch me, I haven't told God yet.'

The seventies were a time of tremendous activity. Jimmy was teaching in Andover, teaching history at our local comprehensive school and apart from taking his history lessons he was also Head of House. He took his pastoral work very seriously and made a point of visiting the home of every child in his house. He had his own private code for grading the parents; those who went on watching the T.V., those who turned it down and the few who turned it off.

Looking back on some of my Christmas round robin letters, I see that we entertained well over a hundred people at the beginning of one year. We had a party for all his staff and their husbands and wives and parties for his badge holders, or prefects. My recipe for these parties was non-stop games and as much food as they could eat. But four years running we took on some major activities. We had a Shakespeare play in the garden, Jimmy organised a civil war battle in the park given by the Sealed Knot Society, we made the cottage the venue for a wedding of a member of his staff and we held a Son et Lumiére behind the church to celebrate the Queen's Silver Jubilee. Added to these activities, I wrote a nativity play for the whole of my school and much of our spare time was spent in driving backwards and forwards to Sussex and Bedfordshire, because both sets of parents were becoming increasingly frail and we tried to prop them up in every way.

We put on a *Midsummer Night's Dream* three nights running in our lower garden, boarding over the pond to make a stage. We used the zigzag path for the fairies to lead on Jimmy, taking the part of Bottom in a donkey's head and for Vicky, taking the part of Puck, to put a girdle round the earth in forty minutes. It was a charming production and the play divided itself easily into three parts for the rehearsals. One night it would be the Greek court, mostly composed of our friends in the village or nearby. One night it was the clowns who included most of the Parish Council and the third night we had the fairies Bottom, Titania and Oberon and most of Class II. The fairies for reasons I really cannot remember, needed feeding and so it was our busiest rehearsal night and over the production the whole cottage was taken over. The props were housed in my burrow, the lighting in the kitchen, the dining room became a long green room, and all the cottage bedrooms were used for dressing rooms and makeup. Meg and Peg our much loved next-door neighbours were in charge of making coffee in Jimmy's workroom at the end of the dining room.

I told the entire cast that they were free to go anywhere except the drawing room but one rather rude mechanical considered this suggestion did not apply to him. He took his greasepaint into the drawing room to make himself up, dropped it and then trod on it. I found him and his wife rather trying, because they had experience of amateur dramatics and we had not, so they considered the props, such as the donkey's head were not part of their costume arrangements. There was a tense moment when Shirley in charge of costumes removed Titania's dress from her dressing room without telling her and everybody came under suspicion. But we were universally united in our irritation with the producer. He was gay and a sad little man who had been given the job to cheer him up, but he hugged his problems to himself and was so self satisfied that I discovered an Amazon in the kitchen taking careful aim at him with her bow. Our other problem was the character of Lion who had to be taken away to be dried out in hospital with an alcohol problem. I recall we had a different Lion for each production but it turned out very well and we had a most encouraging write-up from the critic of the Roundhouse Theatre.

In 1975, the Sealed Knot Society re-enacted the Battle of Andover 1644, in the fields adjoining the Convent. Jimmy who was an old friend of Peter Young, who started the Sealed Knot, was chairman of the organising committee besides undertaking all the publicity, liasing with the Sealed Knot and raising £3,000 worth of guarantees in case of bad gates and other possible disasters. I canvassed the village for the same reason and, apart from a small number of local people who spread alarm and despondency claiming that the nuns would be raped and all the houses of the village pillaged, which didn't help our blood pressure in the run up to the event, it really was a great success. We had 2,000 performers camping very peacefully in the village and it was delightful to see small parties of cavaliers strolling along the village street and watch the opposing armies forming up on the playing field in their seventeenth century uniforms. We were terribly lucky with the weather and over the two days the 1,400 spectators brought in over £5,000. So £1,000 went to form a village trust fund while £600 was given to other charities.

During the interval on the first day, the Tedworth Hounds made an appearance. They had been raised by Mr. Assheton Smith when he was living at the house, which later became a convent and on the second day there was a free fall parachute display by the Royal Green Jackets. Jimmy and I were kept pretty busy. We had a party for 100 Cavaliers on our lawn one night and we found ourselves rounding up the cattle and putting paper in the portable lavatories the next night. Even the winding up seemed to take several weeks. I remember Jimmy's voice coming over the loud speaker reciting a poem by Will Olgilvie when the hounds poured across the field. A feeling of mixed emotions came over me, pride, happiness and a certain knowledge that this was a high peak in our lives that would never come again. However, it was the next year that we put on a Son et Lumière behind the village church to honour the Queen's Jubilee.

I was able to write the script, because of Jimmy's historical knowledge and every child in our small school took part, as well as about thirty from Jimmy's school who performed dances for the Wars of the Roses and the Civil War. The lights were focused on the back of our small 14th century church but we based the action from the reign of Edward III when the church was built to the present day. Every reign had a scene played by the children doing a mime, or playing a game, they might have played at that time. Miss B. had made some really stunning costumes and we dressed the children in one pew and put them to sit and not wriggle in the pew behind. Senior children made their base in the choir stalls and the vestry was set apart as a loo with our ancient commode. We also had a large back screen projector showing slides of episodes in that period and Willie Scambler our dear farmer friend and I had a fascinating morning choosing suitable music for the different reigns. Everything worked so well and the result was excellent, but there are always some who will try and destroy something worthwhile.

One hour before we were about to begin, Jimmy was in the bath and I was making final adjustments to the mini stage with a member of Jimmy's staff, when we discovered to our horror that the lighting had been sabotaged and the slides muddled. Later we found that the electrical cable had been cut through with a knife in parts. Thanks to an excellent electrician and John Scicluna who kindly supported me, we had everything repaired and running in time, but it all seemed so pointless and unkind. We were forced to have another show in the village hall later, to make some money for replacing the cable lent to us by a kind electrician friend. But the children were true professionals and did their parts charmingly, even the five-year old who had sudden nerves at having to walk out into a darkened churchyard. Miss B gave her a sharp push in the back she walked out into the dark.

What else happened in the seventies? Jimmy's mother had died peacefully with all her family around her, just before we went to college in 1964 and in the early seventies, we lost our beloved Nunky, Jack Wills. At the end of the seventies, Dad died after a miserable confused end, which he certainly did not deserve. During our forty-two years of married life, Jimmy had to arrange seven family funerals and the disposal of five family houses and I once made the awful gaffe of greeting the local undertaker with the words, 'How nice to see you again.'

Death is never anything but sad, even for the most hardened criminal who has no chance to redeem himself, or the dearly loved person who has had to endure so much suffering. I shall never understand suffering, especially of the young and innocent. Perhaps we are not meant to in this life. Our Lord had to endure every form of suffering; persecution, poverty, being forced to become a refugee, hardship, being completely misunderstood by all those around him, betrayed by a close friend, injustice, torture and horrendous death in order that we might be forgiven and be shown how to live.

No, there is nothing amusing about death, but in the case of the Robertson family, the various funerals all had a faintly humorous side. Jimmy's mother had wanted to be scattered on Romney Marsh where many years before she and Nunky had had a very happy picnic.

We were five altogether on the scattering party; Jimmy's father and uncle and sister, Jimmy and myself. Scattering Mum's ashes was quite straightforward, but then came the complication of the casket. Jimmy's sister who was never very practical thought it would be nice to keep it but this idea was firmly turned down and the men of the party decided to sink it in a nearby dyke. In our emotional state we had all forgotten that wood floats and it had to be retrieved and filled up with stones, but there was one anxious moment when the men folk made a human chain down the side of the dyke in their attempt to sink it. Jimmy being the most agile was nearest the water, holding on to the hand of Nunky who had one stiff leg from a polo accident, and Jimmy's father was anchor man at the top of the dyke as he had lost a leg and an eye in the First World War. Nobody got wet but it was a very near thing.

When Nunky died, Jimmy and I set out on our own to the same spot after collecting the ashes from the undertaker. I remember saying to Jimmy as I held the parcel on my knee in the car, 'Darling, Nunky is red hot.' 'Nonsense,' said Jimmy. 'I expect they left him on a radiator.' We were driving in Nunky's lovely old Rover car, which we had been lent for our honeymoon and we suddenly became aware that we were being shadowed by a police car. At some time in her distant past, the Rover had been stolen by a criminal gang who were dealing in drugs and due to some clerical error the number plate had never been taken off the police's suspicious list. I can't think why we felt so guilty, perhaps because we never asked anybody's permission to scatter ashes on that spot. But as we scrambled through a wire fence watched by the eye of the law we opened Nunky's parcel in a tearing hurry and a brisk wind from the marsh covered us with ash as if we had been at work on a bonfire. Knowing Nunky, he probably did it on purpose.

When his father died, Jimmy invited Mr. Sechiari the elderly family solicitor back for lunch, as well as the representative of the

Royal Bank of Scotland who travelled down from London for the funeral. His father and his housekeeper had moved into a comfortable bungalow in the village a few weeks before, but it was set in a farmyard and the representative from the bank must have had a tiresome job to remove the Sussex mud from his patent leather shoes when he returned to the West End on an afternoon train. But the lunch was good and somewhat hilarious because we were all so overwhelmingly thankful that Dad's suffering was over. After his third glass of wine, Mr. Sechiari announced to the gathering around the table, 'I was just thinking of your ancestor who was eaten by cannibals.' Apparently, many years before, a member of the family had been captured on a remote Pacific island. As the cooking pot was coming up to the boil, great-great Uncle Matthew was given a choice. Either he could have the Chief's daughter in marriage or she could have him for dinner. Our great, great Uncle must have been the kind of man that made the Empire great. He took one look at the Chief's daughter and murmuring 'Floreal Etona' he chose the pot.

For some years, the family also held the deeds of ownership to a Pacific Island. It was a lovely thought but it would have taken at least a gunboat to reclaim it.

After the funeral, Jimmy and I set about sorting Dad's clothes. We had to work fast because the housekeeper's little boy had been ill and needed to return to his mother. I made three piles; to keep, to give away, and to burn. When I came to Dad's Home Guard uniform, I did not hesitate. I ran down the garden path to where Jimmy was burning Dad's artificial leg on the bonfire. As I handed Jimmy the uniform, he had the sense to shake the canvas shoulder bag. It was packed with live ammunition.

Jimmy and I always claimed the only unkind thing that Nunky ever did was to leave us to look after Aunt Doris. Aunt Doris had quarrelled with her father who had been a doctor (and thought it was unwise for her to marry her first cousin), she had quarrelled with

Jimmy's mother, presumably because she had agreed with the father, and Nunky and poor Aunt Mona who died young were far too kind to quarrel with anyone. I can't imagine why Uncle Tom was drawn to Aunt Doris but being a sailor he may not have given himself time to look around. He was a very successful sailor who was tremendously popular with his contemporaries. Even when he became an Admiral, his after dinner party piece was to eat a wineglass. Whether this eventually gave him cancer, I do not know but he was buried at sea after a full naval funeral. Aunt Doris certainly had a great sadness in her life. Her only son, Collingwood, died as a teenager and his sister Val followed him before her twentieth birthday. Some people accept their grief and sometimes turn it around to help others in distress but Aunt Doris clasped her sorrows to her and became a lonely and embittered old lady.

Nunky was angelic to her and if he ever took her to the theatre he would see the play for himself first in case there was any mention of the Navy or little girls called Val. On the only occasion he failed to do so, he was horrified to find the heroine was called Val and the hero a dashing naval officer. When Nunky died, Jimmy took on the responsibility of seeing that she was being cared for in her dark, depressing little home in Worthing. But she refused all help and even drove Jimmy's sister away with a broom when she called to give her some flowers. I think we may often tell a lot about a person's character by looking at the books they read and Aunt Doris' was not a happy one. *Come Let Us Hate* was one depressing volume together with *Mein Kampf* and *Hitler's Women*. Surprisingly she did have a copy of Jeffrey Farnol's *Chronicles of an Imp*. But I discovered that the night nurse had taken that away with her.

I had just had my tonsils out, so I was unable to go to the funeral. Aunt Doris had provided her own gravestone sometime before, leaving just enough room for the date. A photograph of this memorial hung in her bedroom. Jimmy was furious when he discovered that she had given orders that Uncle Tom's naval sword should be buried in her coffin. 'What a bloody waste,' he exclaimed. But when we started to clean up the little house, we found that she was a failed authoress and she had written several poignant songs. One composition declared: *I am the tiercel, you are the dove, poor little you.* But even more astonishing was the discovery of twenty-six white china chamber pots all neatly wrapped up in brown paper. William came with us for this expedition and he was so disturbed by the atmosphere that he cocked his leg in every room.

The last of his family to go was Jimmy's sister, who was brave and intelligent and very attractive, but she could be a mixed blessing for she always attempted to bully Jimmy. When she was a small girl she had thrown a flat iron at him. She lived for her cats and her horses and, like many people who like horses, she was not concerned with the cleanliness of her kitchen, so most of the cups and cooking utensils were edged with cat fur. Unfortunately, we only found the switch for the immersion heater the day before we left, so all the water had to be heated in a kettle. We also had a double treasure hunt to find the money she had told a friend she had hidden under her carpet and to identify the early warning equipment, which was in her charge as a member of the civil defence. We were not sure who the enemy was supposed to be but we gathered together an assorted range of aerials and mysterious boxes, which we discovered under the beds and cupboards.

Margaret had shown great courage when she returned from hospital for a week's preparation before facing another operation for cancer. In that time she had finalised her will and overlooking the fact that Jimmy had arthritis and was not always steady on his feet, she expressed a wish that her brother should scatter her ashes on the top of Willmington Hill overlooking her village and her old home. Willmington Hill must be one of the highest points of the South Downs. The morning of the funeral was bright and sunny but by the time we set out on our mission that afternoon a steady drizzle was falling and the only happy member of the party was Vicky, the beloved yellow Labrador who had replaced William. We climbed and we climbed and the path became steeper and ever more slippery. I then became aware that Jimmy was pulling himself up on his hands and knees. I told him we were being ridiculous, that we had found a delightful spot where Margaret would have a beautiful view of all the places she loved and we had better scatter her quickly before one or both of us broke an ankle. I then slipped and sat down heavily on my bottom while the empty container careered down the hill followed by an enthusiastic Vicky.

A week after our return home, I woke up one morning with a trapped nerve in my leg. My clever osteopath clicked me back into shape when he returned from his holiday, but it took several painful weeks to recover completely. One night, finding I could not sleep I abandoned Jimmy and tiptoed into his dressing room in search of a softer mattress. I had forgotten his passion for the Stuarts. At the foot of the bed was a picture of the scaffold at Whitehall and below it two pictures given to him by an old friend who had just moved into a nursing home. 'The Dying Cavalier' and the marble effigy of Princess Elizabeth, eldest daughter of Charles I. With a squeak of pain I sank back on my pillow only to hit my head on an imposing picture of Charles I being mocked by the Parliamentary soldiers. Anyway, the mattress was an improvement.

CHAPTER THIRTEEN

Requiem

~~~~~~

1979 was another watershed, for I had been aware for some time that our school numbers were getting lower and lower and one can not expect to go on teaching a small class when the town schools are bursting at the seams. It was a case of last in first out and I was the one to be re-deployed. I was given a choice of three schools in Andover and Jimmy drove me round each one. We both decided that the Church of England School looked the nearest we could find to a village school. Jimmy was convinced I would be happiest there. Once again, I found myself teaching in a temporary classroom but this time I had thirty-seven, seven to eight year olds. They had had little experience of discipline and for my first two terms, I constantly wondered if I could survive.

But things improved and the seven years I spent at East Street were extremely happy ones. The staff were all wonderfully kind and after that first awful year the children were angelic. Jimmy always claimed that children could be very much like hounds, they have to get used to you. Did they come out with some unforgettable remarks? Of course they did. I should really have kept a notebook to remember them but I recall two anyway. An archaeologist is a man who digs for Roman Catholics and the Roman Army had to leave this country because Rome was being attacked by ball bearings.

A few months after my move into Andover, this time without William who was getting rheumaticky and certainly would have not been welcome by any town school, we had another major family crisis. My parents had both celebrated their eightieth birthdays in

1979 and my mother thankfully had been able to keep her birthday with her twin brother, which was a great achievement.

We had all been wondering for some time what to give my mother and her twin for their eightieth birthday, for what can you give two beloved people to show them how much you love them? Then, in the middle of the snow, the winter before, Libby Dampier Child decided to go to Cambridge to take a course on heraldry. Libby was fast approaching eighty herself and she lived in a fairytale thatched cottage in our village. Her hair remained dark auburn until she died and in trying to describe her to my cousin David I told him she was a mixture of Auntie Mamie, Margaret Rutherford and the fiercest admiral in the fleet. I should explain that her father had been a Lieutenant-Commander in the Navy but he had tragically drowned at sea. To commemorate her link with the Navy the first thing you saw on entering her cottage was a framed picture of Lord Nelson reverently draped in the White Ensign.

After thirteen years as headmistress of a small primary school on Salisbury Plain, she retired with an OBE and a desire to take a degree at the Open University. Of course she passed with honours and although she had taken on the task of unpaid curate to our overworked Rector, she still found herself with time on her hands. Hence the heraldry course, hence the first idea for the book, for David had the only copy of the family tree, and if Libby could copy it he agreed it would be an ideal present to give the twins. Furthermore, he heroically offered to have Libby's work photocopied so that every member of the family could have their own copy. This entailed various crises, which varied from the late delivery of a plate-making processor (the only operator capable of dealing with such work developing a boil on his bottom) and the temporary loss of a whole section of the family tree, which turned up in a pile of artwork on the layout artist's desk.

Once Libby had embarked upon the work of recording the various Doctons, Kempthorns and Martyns, the telephone between the cottages was seldom silent.

'Darling I can't quite read the writing... do you think William Martyn married a Mary or Maria in 1701?'

'Libby darling, I don't know, do you want me to look at the book with you tonight?'

'Well, it might be an idea and I can't make out Granny James, the family goes all around the page; was her father married twice?'

'No, but they would have taken up some room, there were twelve of them.'

'Oh well no wonder and when you come I can give you some lettuce and sweet peas from the garden.'

Although my knowledge of my maternal relatives increased over the months my knowledge of heraldry was hazy to say the least and I tiptoed through a maze of heraldic terms with cautious faltering steps. Lions became rampant, helmets were mantled, supporters had

1984. Andover Church of England Primary School,
East Street. Class 4 Form photograph

1983. Andover Church of England Primary School, East Street. Class 4 hard at work.

sinister ermines and as for gouttes, Great Uncle Henry had some very smart gouttes but alas we could not discover their colour. They could have been red, rather gory but a contrast to so much legal black, they could have been gold better still, or they could have been pitch black. I suggested to Libby that we made it up and it took two glasses of sloe gin to revive her. So she then appealed to the Lancaster Herald of Arms. He immediately dropped his portcullis and demanded a ransom. I explained the dilemma to David and was a little disappointed that he did not carry out a James Bond – or do I mean Robin Hood – raid on the College of Arms after dark. I think it would have done them good. Nevertheless, David produced the answers in record time. We were all in total ignorance of the fact that all the relevant information was hanging up on the wall in Uncle Pip's downstairs cloakroom.

Sometime after the twins' eightieth birthday, we found Libby in great distress. Her precious cat Nicolette, had died. Jimmy buried

Nicolette in her garden but Libby continued to mourn and grieve and we decided something had to be done. Class two had informed me that there was a very good kitten shop quite near to the school and we made our way there on a wet Saturday morning. We were introduced to a charming diminutive kitten, which must have been far too small to leave its mother. 'Is it a girl?' I enquired. 'Oh yes,' replied the rather gormless youth who was holding the fort for the owner of the shop. She sat on my lap in the car gazing with fascination at the busy windscreen wipers and we carried her tenderly into Libby's cottage and told her we had found her in the hedge. Libby squeaked with excitement and immediately pulled out all her 'how to look after your cat' books. The kitten behaved impeccably, using the ash box and eating well and Libby was comforted.

As it was coming up to Remembrance Sunday, Libby announced that she would call her new infant Poppy. Libby often wrote notices for the postman or passing friends and pinned them to her gate, such as: Dear Postman, I'm up the garden, please put parcel on kitchen table. This time the notice read: Dear Postman, please shut the gate in case Poppy gets out. A few weeks passed and Poppy was taken to the vet for her injections and general check-up. The vet turned Poppy upside down and then smiled. 'I'm sorry but this is no Poppy,' he said. The next day the notice read: Dear Postman, please shut the gate in case Poppy (this was crossed out in black ink) EARL HAIG (inserted in capital letters) gets out. But everybody agreed that Earl Haig was too much of a mouthful and the kitten was called Poppit.

Jimmy and I could see that my parents were becoming more and more frail. Twice I had had to take leave from my school because my mother had to have a minor operation and D was at last waking up to reality. We had found the perfect companion for them, tactful, capable and gentle, who had cared for their greatest friends for years, but D was in an obstinate, independent mood. 'Just understand old girl, I will never have another woman in my house.' It was maddening and really very worrying, as there was nothing else we could do. Jimmy and I always loved our visits to my parents for we never seemed to stop laughing. Jimmy had become their most beloved son and D and he had so much in common with hunting and country things and my mother kept their little house as neat and as shiny as the best kept doll's house. She was remarkable in her care of D and when he had finished a long, happy day picking up she would drive her mini out to the farm house where he was having an after-shoot tea with his men friends and collect Brock, his last yellow Labrador and probably the best he ever had, so that she could take him home and dry and feed him after his long day of picking up. And when D returned home she would gather up all his shooting clothes and brush them and scrub them and polish them, all ready for his next outing. And here I have to be strictly honest; she once made him undress in the field. Perhaps this was because she had once discovered two very dead moorhens in his shooting coat.

But now the sands were running out and my mother had to be whisked into hospital again with what turned out to be septicaemia. Poor darling D had had to spend several hours on his own before I reached him at midday the next day and the father who collected me at the station was a changed man. He had heated up a thermos of soup to greet me and he was full of plans on how to re-arrange the furniture and how to find someone to care for him and my mother when she came out of hospital. I think it was one of the low points in my life because I was being pulled in two directions. Jimmy was understanding and patient, but naturally my school wanted me back and I could not find anyone who would take on the task.

D would drive me into the hospital in his Land Rover. 'Stand up over the bumps, old girl,' while Brock who had a keen imagination would sit beside me with his head tucked up under my arm so he could not see the road. D would start the journey by taking an angina pill. He would take another one in the hospital car park and another one when he reached the third floor where Mummie was in bed near the door. I would steal a chair for him from one of the nurse's offices but I always wondered if I would have to leave him in the bed next to my mother. Mercifully, my guardian angel came up trumps as usual and a very sweet retired nurse who lived in a nearby village agreed to come in everyday and look after them so that I could return home. This was all due to the kindness of the headmaster of the school, where D was Chairman of Governors.

In 1979, there was no official backup for people in our situation and I had made fifty telephone calls before I found Beryl, who has remained our friend ever since. We had always expected we should lose my mother first but as it happened, D was the first to go and, although he had become increasingly breathless over the months, it came as a tremendous shock to me when I was told that he had collapsed and died on his way to the bathroom only forty-eight hours after we had left them after Christmas. My mother just like granny, was wonderful in a crisis and when we arrived a few hours later she just said, 'Darlings, I want to come home with you.' I still wonder to this day, how Jimmy organised everything so well in such a short time. Apart from all the formalities, he took D's cremation service himself.

My father had been a sincere and thinking Christian but he was suspicious of any form of priest craft, being certain that he could approach his maker very humbly on his own. D had previously had some horrendous plan for his funeral. His coffin was to be followed by a huntsman with a leash of hounds, a fisherman with his rod, a man with his gun and presumably his Labrador and a falconer with a bird on his hand. I imagine he took note of our horrified faces when he briefly proposed this awesome cortége, because in his last will there was no mention of it, he just left it all to James. His service was completely private as he wished and after my mother died, we had a thanksgiving service for both of them.

But apart from the funeral and the official notices there was Pickfords to be contacted, for we had just one week to move my mother back to our cottage with all her things and we would have about two days before they arrived to dispose of a greater part of our things, to leave room for Mummie's furniture. Being an only child, I knew the family furniture would come to me one day, so we had made vague plans as to where all the pieces would go and this proved invaluable. When we were burgled a few years before, we had lost all our silver and all my jewellery and instead of replacing them we had spent the insurance money on extending the dining room and this again was a tremendous help. In the few days before he had to return to school, Jimmy spent his time erecting two large cupboards, one in the kitchen and one in the dining room to take my mother's things.

My main task was to find carers from the village to come and be with her while we were at school, for the doctors had told me that she must never be left alone. We live in a very caring village, and I found my team. It may have been a coincidence, but my shift rota included a Heather, a Violet, a Phyllis (philodelphus), Mary Withers, Nellie Flowers and Sheila Green.

Another problem was that our two dogs, William and Brock did not get on. William had once told D he was a lovely man and Brock had replied by telling William to keep off because D belonged to him, and he had pushed William into a thorn bush. William never forgot this injustice and it could have been dynamite to let them meet. We kept up the separation for six months, each dog having his own end of the house with the dining room as 'no man's land.' And then Jimmy said, 'I can't take this any longer,' and accompanied by Henry our gardener we let them both off the leads in a field where, after a rather terse conversation in which William told Brock quite firmly that he was top dog and Brock must call him sir, peace reigned. William was a personality and after that he insisted on climbing Mummie's staircase and knocking his head on her glass door. He would then throw himself expansively at my mother's feet while she gave him a chocolate drop. Meanwhile Brock, who was half William's size, would sit with a pained expression gazing at the ceiling.

It took some time to get the cottage straight and it was difficult when I had to return to school because after Pickfords arrived with two and a half vanloads, I found myself with two of everything. Two ironing boards, two washing up bowls, two hoovers – the dining room and my study looked like a storeroom. Luckily, Sheila, or Cinders as we called her, brought her father's car and we loaded it up with all the extra kitchen equipment, for the Weyhill Seniors' jumble sale.

I put Mummie in charge of sorting and tidying the cupboards, with the help of one of her floral carers. I knew she would do it beautifully because she was so tidy and well organised and I thought it might help her to come to terms with losing D. The shock for her must have been appalling. One moment she was captain of her own ship, the next she had lost much of her independence; but it all worked out in time.

I think that one of the happiest memories I have of Mummie was when she and I were sitting in the garden while she helped me make out name tags for each child in class two to stick above their coat hooks. I could not give her grandchildren, but when I brought the children home to the cottage to celebrate William's birthday in the garden, and I saw her surrounded by class two I felt she had the next best thing.

Sometime before my mother came to live with us Jimmy became involved with the organisation of the sponsored walk for Save the Children. At first it was a school house project, but after the elderly Colonel, who had been organising it retired, Jimmy took the whole thing over. We aimed at having a thousand walkers a year and over the years, he was responsible for bringing in over £100,000. My primary school followed his lead and I found that in many ways it was more convenient teaching in Andover. I could buy things in my lunch hour for my mother and collect her medicines. And when I needed to bank the Save the Children takings I would take them into school in the morning in a yellow bag at the bottom of my shopping trolley and slip down to the bank at 12 o'clock.

One Wednesday I made my usual trip to Lloyd's Bank, greeted the cashier with 'Here we come again, Save the Children' and plunged my hand into the bottom of the trolley to find to my horror there was no yellow bag. Feeling rather sick I telephoned Jimmy.

'Did you put the bag into my trolley this morning?'

'Yes,' he replied. 'There were seven cheques and over a £100 pounds in cash.'

Jimmy told me he would stop the cheques and I returned to school. My headmaster was equally horrified and when the children were told they spent the rest of their playtime looking for Mrs Robertson's yellow bag in the most unlikely places. Mr Sillence then told me he would take my sewing class while Margery, my dear friend

July 1990. Cheque for Save the Children Fund, given by Farleigh School.

and school secretary, took me down to the police station to make a statement. Of course the money was never recovered: Jimmy made it up and I realised how stupid I had been.

There was one child in my class who came from a notorious family. His older brothers had all spent time at Her Majesty's expense and his sisters had only one career in mind. Their mother was a massive woman with scraped-back hair in a large bun and she always made me think she must have been the original camp follower. John was a nice child who drew beautifully, and I am glad to say he went on to become a capable draftsman, but at the age of eight he was being groomed like Fagin's Artful Dodger. When he offered to stay in and sharpen the pencils, I simply thought he was being thoughtful, little thinking he was casing the joint. The only time my trolley was out of my sight was during assembly, when we all gathered in the hall and it would have been easy for one of the family to walk into the classroom with a Mars bar for John's break and help themselves to the yellow bag. We could never prove anything, but it seemed more than a coincidence that the whole family spent the day in Bournemouth the following week.

I think John's mother may have had a twinge of conscience, for one afternoon in the middle of a lesson, the door burst open and Mrs V appeared on the threshold like one of the Furies. 'Mrs. Robertson,' she boomed. 'I've brought you a present,' and she gave me a brand new copy of *The Diary of an Edwardian Lady*. Where it came from I prefer not to think, but it was a very kind thought.

On another occasion, we had an invasion of travellers who took over the car park next to my classroom. About thirty caravans parked alongside of us and as it was a very wet day, the owners of the caravans claimed that all the children needed schooling. One heroic teacher was given the job of teaching them, but we all increased our vocabulary and it was inevitable there was an outbreak of nits. When Mummie heard that I had nits, she was electrified and far from collapsing from shock, she sat up in bed with various wild suggestions that the curtains and everything in the cottage would have to be fumigated. Admittedly, I had been a little shocked myself when I saw my hairdresser silently poised over my scalp like a pointer winding a covey of partridges. Then I suffered the humiliation of being returned to the basin while the apprentice was dispatched to the chemist in dark glasses to ask for a special shampoo.

My mother lived with us for three years before she died. Her health gradually deteriorated and she was confined to bed, sometimes needing two carers at a time. I shall always remember her saying, ' I'm getting too much for you darlings, you ought to put me into hospital.' But Jimmy told her quite firmly, 'No Mum, you're staying here at home with us,' and I was so thankful for that. Over that time I discovered it is not always sensible to protect elderly people from shocks. We tried to shield my mother from dogfights and things that go bump in the night, fearing she might have a fatal heart attack. But in actual fact the odd drama acted like a tonic and filled her with interest. I remember Henry's comment about the goldfish when Jimmy had to lower the depth of water to carry out a repair on the lining of the pond. 'Probably do them a power of good,' he remarked. 'My old father used to say, take a stick and stir up the water a bit, they get so scared they flush themselves through and they are twice as frisky after that.' Henry has looked after our garden for about twenty-five years and he is rich in the wisdom of the countryside.

But we had one drama, which could not be hidden from my mother. One evening a young motorist skidded around our corner on one wheel, collided with Meg's fence opposite us and then ricocheted back onto our dining room wall cracking it from floor to ceiling, but luckily not damaging the Bristol blue glass which stood on an old family table. Hearing the crash, I thought Mummie had fallen out of bed, but she was sitting up looking rather astonished. It was Jimmy who found the uninsured, untaxed car imbedded in the wall, with its lights still on and the keys in the ignition. The police arrived complete with police dog, which obligingly found a glove.

The driver turned out to be one of Jimmy's pupils who had fled up the road when he realised which house he had run into.

It took a little time for the travellers to receive their eviction order, but one day the class teacher in the next room to mine burst in with the good news. 'June, they are going!' And they were as silently as migrating swallows. Their great caravans rolled away, leaving only their litter to remind us of times past. Shortly after this I was giving Class II a spelling test. It was a peaceful half hour with heads bent, legs gently swaying, pencils gripped in hot hands, faces intent with tremendous effort and then a sudden exclamation from Michael, ' Cor, Miss, they are mating!' My hair rose on my scalp. Oh no! I was sure all the travellers had left the car park. I glanced fearfully out of the window and there were two innocent blackbirds preparing for their family of china blue eggs.

Around 1985 – Jimmy & Vicky

I was thankful I was not ordered to give sex instruction to Class II. The middle juniors had quite enough to occupy them anyway. Only once, when I was teaching in my first country school, I was asked to spell the word 'castration' for a child who had been helping his farming uncle in the holidays.

Mummie died peacefully at home with us in February 1984 and in 1985 Jimmy retired from teaching. He would drive me into school every morning, hand me my books over the wire from the car park and then drive on to take Brock and Vicky for a walk. Brock, D's beloved little Labrador, was our comforter now and he lived to be nearly seventeen. We also had Vicky who was chosen and trained for us by Shirley and Derrick Berridge. Derrick had been one of the head keepers on the estate where D used to shoot and pick up and when we collected Vicky we knew it was the start of a lifelong friendship for they were the kindest dearest couple. It worked out well but I knew I was becoming more and more tired.

After my mother died, I picked up various bronchial infections and the day came when I found reading *Little Grey Rabbit* to a class of enchanting six years olds left me completely shattered and I put in for early retirement. My colleagues warned me that the doctor who would be interviewing me disliked service wives and could be abrupt, but he turned out to be kind and understanding. 'Do you ever cry, Mrs. Robertson?' and I had to admit that I did. I left school for the last time just before Christmas in 1986 and looking back, I am glad that Jimmy and I had that time together before life started to run downhill. We spent a wonderfully happy holiday in Ireland in 1989 when we explored, for the first time, the ruins of the old family home Lissen Hall. In 1994 my book, *A Long Way From Tipperary* was published in which I told the story of D's Irish family. I wondered at one time whether I should include the last years of Jimmy's life, but this is a true story and birth and death are all part

1989. First visit to Lissen Hall ruins – Jimmy & Donal Gleeson.

of life's experience and I know I learned so much and met so many compassionate people during the next ten years.

I would think that most people tell themselves when I retire I will do that job and that task which has been pending for so long. I know that was true of Jimmy because he was always full of plans and he was never tired of making the cottage more comfortable and more convenient, but he found his physical strength was failing. He was one of the first officers in the Middle East to catch polio during the war and he had spent his twenty-first birthday in hospital in Cairo. His only present had come from a young American who was working for the Red Cross at that time. Jimmy was lucky because, unlike so many who developed polio, he appeared to make a complete recovery, only having a slight stiffness in one leg if he had been driving for many hours.

He passed a parachuting course, he trained with the Commandos, he whipped in to hounds, he was always thinking up endless tests for his soldiers that would enable them to get fitter and increase their morale. He undertook every conceivable building task in the cottage. Returning from a village jumble sale one day, I discovered him halfway up a ladder carrying a new bath on his back, which he was putting into our new second bathroom. But as the years passed that strength was ebbing and the power in his arms and legs was becoming weaker. We consulted specialists but they had no comfort to give, except to use a walking stick as a third leg. As the days passed, we went through the various stages. We installed a Stannah lift when he fell, and found it almost impossible to get up; we installed a Parker bath, which transformed getting in and out of the bath and our first carer was a sweet woman who came to supervise his bath, because I realised I would not have the strength to help him.

For about two years some sweet friends in the village allowed us to use their indoor swimming pool and that was a wonderful help, but that in time became an expedition fraught with possible crisis.

1994 The launch of "A long way from Tipperary"
at Hammicks Bookshop, Andover.

Once he lost his footing in the bath and it was fortunate I was beside him to pull him up to the surface. But getting into the water was a constant worry, as there was no hand rail and Jimmy had to go down the steps backwards hanging on to his Zimmer frame, which I held at the top. The crisis came when he slipped coming out of the water and fell across a rowing machine, breaking a chair on the way down. It had all become too difficult and poor Jimmy lost his treat of the week. But to me far more worrying than the countless falls, which turned my tummy into a permanent knot was the fact that his concentration and reaction was slowing down. And at times when he awoke he had become utterly confused thinking we were painting our bedroom or having a cocktail party and once becoming worried that we had not signed up for our courses at college.

I think my first reaction was anger. Why could he not wake up from this dream and talk sense? Why could I not communicate with my dearest friend who would always tell me what to do? But the doctor explained that Jimmy had had a series of minor strokes and I must just go along with it and humour him. So when he began worrying about the time term started at college, I went into the kitchen, counted to ten and returned to tell him that I had signed us both on for the new term. 'What day does that start?' he asked. '21 September,' I replied as it was the first day that came into my head.

Of course, there were glimpses of sunlight in a darkening landscape. While Jimmy had been fighting over the Nijmegen area in the war, he had needed some scrap paper to make a fire plan. He had walked into the local school and picked up a child's exercise book. After glancing at the neat writing and carefully drawn botanical pictures, he had decided he could not possibly use it for rough paper and he slipped it into his pack. For years, we kept it with our special treasures and then about the time of the VE Day anniversary, he decided to return it, only to find it had disappeared. However a year later, we discovered it and Jimmy started negotiations with the

Town Hall officials of Nijmegaen to find the owner. They did, and it appeared that the exercise book had belonged to a Mrs. Grada Potjens Teunissan when she was a 15-year old school girl. We were so happy to know she was reunited with her book. We would have kept up with her afterwards, but it was difficult with the language, for we had to find an interpreter to read her letters.

After my book was published in 1994, Jimmy booked two front row seats at the Savoy Theatre to see Susan Hampshire in *Relative Values* and we lunched at the Savoy first in the River Room, which was a wonderful way to celebrate. The Savoy has always seemed a very special place to me. It was there I had my very first dance with D. It had been a long time promise and he had bought me a charming lime green dress and bolero to wear. This had hung on a coat hanger in my bedroom for several weeks and I would give it the occasional stroke. But when I dressed in my room at the Hyde Park Hotel I was devastated to find it had dropped a good two inches all round, having been cut on the cross. D was seldom at a loss and when he saw this disaster he just said, 'Give me some safety pins girl,' and there and then he draped and pinned the hips and the dress was wearable, although it would have been unwise to look too closely. We danced to Carol Gibbon's band. D was a beautiful dancer and I felt very grown up and rather overawed.

The next time I went to the Savoy was for my twenty-first birthday party in '49. I think my parents had made up a party of about twenty and it was a lovely evening. This time I wore a dress of soft pastel coloured brocade, which had been made by friends in Hartnell's workroom. Jimmy was one of the guests and sat on my right with Uncle Bill Slim on my left. Eight years later I dined and danced with Jimmy there when we became engaged and now in '94 we were here again. It was still a delightful hotel, but the glamour seemed to have disappeared in the lunch hour. Instead of frivolous hats the girls at the various tables appeared to have come straight from their offices with black stockings and short skirts and their mobile phones and calculators on the table beside them.

The front row of the stalls was equally unromantic. The woman sitting on my right hand obviously had had a happy morning in the sales. Just before the lights were dimmed and the curtain went up she plunged her hand into her shopping bag and brought out a set of mini Yorkshire pudding tins. They were designed to be fool proof and I was intrigued, but it did not give one a feeling of magic. During the interval, she made another search and this time sat admiring a Peter rabbit mug. The expedition was a great effort for Jimmy and once again my tummy turned itself into knots in case he slipped and fell out of the taxi. London taxis are not very easy for partially disabled people.

In 1997 we had our last celebration for our ruby wedding. We pretended it was to celebrate our time at Rose Cottage, because we did not want our guests to feel forced to bring us presents. Our village amateur dramatic company is excellent and they agreed to put on a production of *The Importance of Being Ernest* two days running in the upper garden. We boarded over the upper pond with scaffolding and planks and we seated a hundred people each day. We were restricted for numbers, because if it had rained everything would have had to be transferred to the village hall, which only seated a hundred. The play was followed by tea, strawberries and cream in the upper garden and besides our friends and family we tried to include all the people who had helped us with the cottage in so many ways over the years. And so the guests included our electrician, postman and farrier as well as our new Labrador puppy's doctor and my hairdresser. It was a happy party because the weather was gloriously sunny almost too hot for the cast. But Jimmy managed it by relying on his Zimmer frame and sticks and he made two charming speeches of thanks to everyone on the two separate days.

After the party, his frailty appeared to increase fairly rapidly and having struggled to get downstairs once a day, he found it was all too difficult and was confined to his room and finally to bed. I was determined to nurse him at home if it was humanly possible and my friends in Social Services assured me that it could be done with help. Due to Jimmy's responsible planning of our financial affairs we now had a little cushion, which I could call upon. But my hardest task was to persuade Jimmy we must have more help. He had always been so wise and full of common sense, but his mind had become confused and I had to almost fight him to agree with my decisions. I found this really distressing because we never quarrelled. There had been the odd growl when I bought him new clothes, but we shared all our thoughts and plans and so much laughter and we always had so much to talk about. We were sometimes amused to watch other married couples having breakfast in a hotel dining room in total silence, while we always had so much to say to each other.

But now, poor darling, he was both confused and frustrated and he withdrew more and more from all around him. He could not understand why we could not cut the bars of his bed and get him up. It was heartbreaking that he should lose his two greatest gifts, his incredible strength and vital energy, always planning something, making something or writing, and now his really remarkable memory had deserted him too. Jimmy could quote much of Shakespeare and Kipling and many other poets, he was a wonderful storyteller, and he could tell you what the weather was like when he fell out of a tree on his seventh birthday. At least he was not in pain, just a helpless prisoner unable to do anything for himself.

But then I think of a sweet friend who was a beautiful needlewoman and who embroidered exquisite frontals for Salisbury Cathedral besides helping many to learn to embroider. At the end of her life she had a stroke and went blind. Why did Beethoven go deaf or Milton blind? We shall not know the answer in this life and

I could not be angry with God. After all, Jimmy had appeared to recover from polio and he had been able to lead an active, happy life unlike so many who had never known the joy of living. Instead, I felt God was very near us, suffering with Jimmy, but I would sit beside the bed and beg for his release. His heart must have been incredibly strong because, for the last fourteen weeks of his life, he survived on syringes of fruit juice and oral morphine. I probably turned him into an addict but it did not matter. He was peaceful and did not suffer.

I was determined to try and behave as normally as possible and so we did not whisper, but laughed and talked around the cottage to try to make him realise he was at home and the situation was not frightening or unusual. I longed to hold him and love him but I made myself into a kind but fairly strict nanny, because I was terrified of breaking down. I knew that then I would be lost, unable to help anybody.

So often the minor crises happened when I was out. Cinders caught me one day at the osteopath to tell me Jimmy was refusing to be washed, so I then spoke to him on the telephone. 'Darling you must be washed, you don't want to be a dirty old man, and then you can have your chicken fricassee for lunch.' I think the waiting room was stunned. Our carers were really wonderful. We had one at 8 o'clock, two at 11, one at 2, one at 6 and then a sleeper in who slept in his dressing room and helped Jimmy in the night when he needed it. I acted as the extra carer when there was only one.

One evening, the carer who appeared at six was Rosemary. She was a sweet, gentle soul but she was only 5ft. tall and when we looked at Jimmy we saw he was completely crooked in his sling having had a session with a district nurse in the afternoon. Rosemary and I looked at him and I told her that we must get him straight for the night, but that I was not going to be much help to her because I had slipped in the kitchen and broken a bone in my shoulder. I decided that I would have to ring for the ambulance, for those crews have a magic knack when it comes to lifting. The girl on the exchange was very kind but not terribly optimistic, for she knew that the ambulance crew had been on duty for twelve hours and fearing that they might let me down she alerted the fire service as well. So, we had one ambulance, and a very smart fire engine flashing their blue lights outside the cottage. Jimmy was just able to take this in and he saw the funny side too.

We turned our bedroom into a single room for him and as we were built into a hill we could walk straight out of his bedroom into the garden filled with birdsong and the sound of the mower on a summer day. Throughout this distressing time I was so desperately grateful for all the help and support we received. My cousin Davina and her brother David were constantly there to support and encourage us. Our friends in the village, particularly Meg and Peg could not have been kinder and more helpful and I had every kind of support from dear Janet Maughan, my Social Services advisor who arranged everything from care to equipment for me.

The mobile hoist proved ineffectual, probably because Jimmy was too heavy for it and we decided to buy our own overhead hoist. I was thrilled and rather surprised when a large lorry laden with steel poles appeared outside the gate one morning a few days after we placed the order for our own hoist. 'Rose Cottage,' cried the driver. 'Yes,' I replied, 'How wonderfully quick you have been.' 'Will you unload it all into the garden,' and I gave him a tip. I telephoned Janet in great excitement. 'Guess what, its arrived,' I told her. 'But June I only placed the order two days ago, have you looked at the invoice?' I looked again and it said Rose Cottage but not our Rose Cottage. The steel poles were destined for Rose Cottage, Penton Grafton where our friend Rod Eggington has his own small garage. So I had to swallow my pride and ring up Rod's son Simon who I had taught at the age of seven and say, 'Simon, I'm terribly sorry but I have been very, very stupid.' Over the years, we received their post and their guests for a firework party and they had been faced with the police and our doctor and a load of manure destined for us. Fortunately, they are our very good friends.

Before Jimmy was confined to bed, I thought it might give him a feeling of independence and freedom if he had an electric buggy, which he could drive around the village. I had persuaded him to give up the car when I realised his reactions were getting slower and it would have been tragic if he had hurt someone, having been such a most competent driver. We bought a smart second hand buggy with a top and the great day came when Jimmy was about to set out. Our garage has two doors back and front, being built into the hill and I think it was entirely my fault that I suggested he drove through the garage uphill and then turned left to come down the hill. It was like a nightmare and I seemed to be watching a slow motion film as I watched him take the corner too closely and the whole buggy tipped over, imprisoning him inside.

I have never felt so helpless, but I heard voices coming from our nearest neighbours up the hill where Ondine was gossiping to Emma. 'Please will you ring for the ambulance,' I cried. 'Jimmy has turned his buggy over.' Ondine, besides being very pretty, was a fast runner and I think she broke the four-minute mile when she ran down the hill to fetch her husband. Hugh appeared within seconds with his brother-in-law and it was nothing short of a miracle that two other extremely kind neighbours appeared at the same time, who had not got bad backs, bad hearts or hernias. They set the buggy upright and got Jimmy out, but we discovered he had broken a rib and the stone marking the telephone cable had missed his head by about an inch.

When we finally had lunch, it consisted of burnt sausages and two very strong gin and tonics.

And what other excitements did we have apart from the odd fall? One day I was being permed in the kitchen and at the vital moment, when the hairdresser has her eyes on her watch to put on the neutraliser, Maria came running down the stairs in some distress. Maria is Spanish and a darling and she slept in two nights a week and also came to watch over Jimmy for an hour in the afternoons. I had left her quite happily upstairs with the district nurse but now she looked distracted. 'Have you got the book of instructions,' she gasped. I bounded up the stairs complete with rollers and there was Jimmy peacefully asleep in his sling, which was resting on the ceiling. I telephoned the engineers but they said it would take them two hours to reach us from Southampton and then I then decided to telephone for the ambulance because we couldn't leave him hanging in mid air. His language when he woke up might be dramatic. The ambulance was setting off when Maria pressed another button and the sling slowly descended to mattress level. But my perm was rather overcooked after that.

Our carers were truly remarkable with only one I found we could not take. But the other ninety-nine percent were kind, patient, caring and I felt as if I was partly an air traffic controller and partly an agony aunt, when I heard about all their backgrounds. I think every known crime and misfortune came into it, rape, abuse, attempted murder, broken homes, love affairs, financial worries. One very sweet carer was weeping into Jimmy's bath water one day telling us about her ex-husband who had turned up out of the blue and was demanding money with menaces. I said, 'Hold on Sally, I'll have a word with Richard who has just come to collect Sophie for a walk. He has retired but he was a top-class solicitor in a city of London practice.' So having obtained my legal advice by the kitchen door I passed it on in the bathroom before Jimmy started to get cold from the addition of so many tears.

I was really happy to attend Sally's wedding to a nice responsible man, which took place in our own small church some months later. But there are some times when, if we had lived in the Middle Ages I would have really believed someone had put the evil eye on us. In one month the mobile hoist broke down seven times and three nights running our kind, elderly electrician came over about ten o'clock at night to put a new fuse into the hoist. This once entailed a visit to our TV engineer in Andover who had the only suitable fuse for the hoist. Added to this the TV broke down, the video went wrong, the lawn mower gave up twice, and the Hoover had to have an appointment with the doctor. Then a nice man arrived to fix the aerial for Jimmy's TV at the bottom of his bed.

After he had left me, we found the telephone had gone dead. I reported the fault but no help appeared. Then Jenny and Bob, who lived two doors up the hill from our cottage, noticed a BT man up the telegraph pole outside their bungalow. They told him our tale of woe and he immediately got onto his mobile phone and called for Pippa. Pippa was young and very pretty and she had no hesitation about shinning up any telegraph pole. We discovered later that she was BT's student of the year. She certainly improved Jimmy's morale and she spent the afternoon crawling about our loft space only to discover that the aerial engineer had put a nail through the telephone wire.

Five hours later Ann arrived to take Jimmy through the night. Ann was faithful and kind, but if anything ever went wrong it always seemed to happen on a Tuesday. She was on duty when Jimmy fell out of bed and stuck himself firmly between his bed and the tallboy. This necessitated calling for Rosy and her ambulance to pull him out like a cork coming out of a bottle. It was Ann who tipped a bucket of water down the stairs and I was always a little nervous of her case when it looked rather full. Ann's husband and son and daughter all kept snakes and when she told me that one had disappeared, I was filled with trepidation, in fact it turned up three weeks later under her bed.

But on this particular Tuesday, Ann did not seem herself and her eyes looked rather glazed. Did she have a migraine? Was she sickening for flu? Or had Jimmy been cross with her? I could get no response from her so I telephoned her home and her daughter answered, 'Coo, Mum has forgotten to take her chocolate.' Up to that moment, I had no idea that Ann was a diabetic but then quite suddenly, she collapsed unconscious on Jimmy's bed. It was no good trying to read her doctor's phone number on her bracelet. This was obviously a case for Rosy and, with my newly mended telephone, I dialled 999. I can't remember how we managed it but somehow I connected Rosy with Ann's husband who was a long distance lorry driver on his way home from Oxford. Rosy then produced an enormous syringe, which she plunged into Ann's arm. It worked but it wasn't quite on target and there was blood everywhere.

However, all was well. Ann was taken home by ambulance and I curled up beside Jimmy for the night.

Our greatest comfort and support was our home team, Vi and Henry and Cinders and of course Stan. Jimmy had taught Stan's twins history and when he first met Stan mending our church roof, it was the beginning of a lifelong friendship. Although Jimmy had been an expert at DIY, as he grew older he had neither the strength nor the time and so it was Stan who relined the pond, Stan who built new steps into the road from the upper garden. He always walked through the door with those infinitely comforting words, 'No problem.' Stan tackled almost any kind of carpentry or brickwork, as well as mending my shoes and repairing a charming little piece of antique china, which had broken into about sixty pieces when it had fallen off a shelf. 'Stan what do I owe you, it's a miracle,' I exclaimed. 'Nothing,' he replied, 'It comes with my love.' He was a miracle worker when it came to Jimmy's needs at the end. He put wooden handles all around the cottage for Jimmy to hold on to, he constructed two ladders for Jimmy to pull himself up, and he extended Jimmy's bed. A neighbour had watched him constructing this wooden extension and had said, 'What are you making now Stan, an owl box?' So the owl box it became.

Cinders and Vi were endlessly kind and patient and caring and they used all their tact and gentleness when Jimmy begged them to release him from his bed and cut through the bars. Meanwhile, Henry, Vi's husband, kept the garden going and was always there when we needed him. One day I had taken a few hours off with Davina, having left Vi and Henry in charge to welcome a new carer. Neil Diamond was coming in for an hour to change Jimmy and massage his feet. I left copious notes telling this stranger who was taking the place of Maria for one afternoon exactly what to do, but unfortunately he arrived with no uniform whatsoever to identify him. He might have come to do the drains, and Jimmy thought he was a confidence trickster and wouldn't allow him to come near him. He refused to be touched. Vi tried to reassure Jimmy that all was well but he was not to be persuaded so she summoned Henry from the garden and Meg from next door. Henry has Romany blood and he was deeply suspicious of Neil, which did not really help and Meg who was a little deaf, could not hear properly on the telephone and was convinced that Rose Cottage was being broken into by confidence tricksters.

I returned home to find the entire cottage in a state of agitation and it took some time to reassure my poor Jimmy. Once he addressed me quite sensibly and calmly. 'When this episode is over,' and I thought, dear God he knows what is happening, he knows he is dying but Jimmy continued, 'When this episode is over wouldn't be a good idea to have a William tea party for all the people who have helped us?' And so I just said, 'Yes darling, what a good idea,' and left it at that. But after he died, I did have a carer's party in the village hall. There could have been over seventy guests but in the end, only thirty-six were free to come but it was a happy party.

Those months of Jimmy's last illness were defiantly the worst of times for us. But amongst all the anxiety and heartache we were aware of being surrounded by so much love and kindness and that made everything bearable. When Mummie was dying I had once said to her,' Darling I think some of us have to go through a Good Friday before we get to Easter,' and I believe that is true. Jimmy died very peacefully in his sleep on the 28 April 2000. It was the Thursday after Easter. They carried him through the French window of his bedroom out onto the top lawn and down steps to the road. It was six o'clock in the morning and the dew still covered the lawn.

2004 Rose Cottage porch.

CHAPTER FOURTEEN

Loose Ends

The sun had filled the garden with light and the only sound was the chorus of bird song. Blackbirds and thrushes, robins and wrens and the soft murmur of the pigeons. They were singing with joy and I cannot believe birds only sing to attract a mate or claim their territory. To me it was a message of hope and resurrection. Now Jimmy was free, now he was safe and I did not need to grieve for him or worry about him anymore. But of course, I did grieve, and the only way to stop myself from breaking down was to follow Jimmy's guidelines on family funerals and keep myself busy.

Some years before, I had said to Jimmy, 'I don't want you to show me every detail but just give me an outline of how you tackle the business things, I don't want to be like Auntie Mamie.' Auntie Mamie had married Uncle Rowland, who you may remember was a clergyman, rather late in life and she became his wife and his child to be cherished and protected from all the harsh realities of life. But when he died, she was completely lost and unnecessarily worried, which did not help her come to terms with losing the love of her life. So, Jimmy instructed me. He was an excellent teacher (not like D, who thought I ought to keep my accounts like the army with double entries. I found it hard to believe D did this himself. It would have taken far too much time away from the Shooting Times.) Jimmy's teaching made things far simpler when he was beginning to find it difficult to concentrate. I know he hated losing his independence, but I tried hard to convince him that I was only doing what he taught me. I was acting as his adjutant and I could always appeal to him if I got stuck.

I am afraid I was once deliberately dishonest and I felt a perfect traitor deceiving him. The conservatory needed new blinds, for the old ones were disintegrating and in danger of breaking and knocking some pretty china off a shelf. I did not choose the cheapest blinds, I had fallen in love with Davina's, which were effective and elegant and hopefully would last for years. I had to admit to Jimmy that I was having new blinds, because I knew he would be wondering what the hammering was under his bedroom. He looked at me fairly sternly and just said, 'How much?' and I told him the cost of the deposit. I hope I am not a natural liar but sometimes white lies save an awful lot of heartache.

The first thing to be done was to restore the cottage to being a home rather than a nursing home. So I sold the overhead hoist back to the firm but kept many of the good grab handles for elderly guests and myself. I had Jimmy's room and bathroom re-papered, there was a new cream carpet to go with the French wallpaper. I kept the Stannah lift and the special bath and I bought a filing cabinet. Everything would be the same and yet different. I also went through all Jimmy's clothes to give away to friends, to give away to charities and to burn. Davina was the greatest help to me and I was happy when many of Jimmy's clothes fitted many of our good friends.

The next thing was to visit Ireland to discuss plans for the final home for the Irish furniture and family treasures. Here, I was supported all the way by Peter and Angela Swift who drove me to Tipperary for a brief but very happy visit. My biggest shock came on my return. I had told Stan I would get him his birthday present in Ireland and he had said, 'Bring me back a leprechaun.' We had made various plans before I left to carry on with a stitch in time policy just as Jimmy would have wished. While I was away, he was going put a new floor in the airing cupboard, which had been rocking like a boat for years and this he did for me.

We stayed with old friends of Peter and Angela in their lovely small stately home just outside Nenagh and at breakfast the next morning Angela asked me, 'Did you have a good night June?' And I replied, 'Yes very good, but I had a frightful nightmare. I dreamed that Stan had died.' We reached home safely and the first thing I heard was that Stan had died of a massive heart attack the day before. It was very hard to take in. I had been expecting to lose Jimmy for so long but I never contemplated losing Stan. Jimmy and I always thought he could have been an archer at Agincourt; in fact he was an archer, strong and sturdy with a wide brow and kindly twinkling eyes and very slightly pointed ears. He had seemed indestructible but we could never take anything for granted and just be ever grateful that our friend, a friend for all seasons helped us for so many years.

Some months before Jimmy died, Davina and her husband Richard invited me to go out to South Africa with them at the end of August, if I found myself on my own by then. My ticket had arrived and I had half packed and cancelled the milk and papers, packed my black Labrador, Sophie for a long stay with Liz and Richard Porter, her favourite walking Aunt and Uncle and then it was discovered that Richard had to go into hospital. It was all very sad and worrying but a blessing that Richard's condition was discovered before we set out and he did not have to go into hospital in Cape Town. The visit was postponed until December but I knew I wanted to get away from everything before then and Davina and Richard suggested that I should spend a week by the sea at Lyme Regis in a hotel they knew well. Just before I set off I developed an infected nerve in my jaw, which made my face look as if I was recovering from mumps. I bit into my first antibiotic and broke a tooth and finally gashed my leg on a taxi door.

Louis and Jackie have been our close neighbours and dear friends for many years and he offered to drive me down for my week's holiday. He was infinitely kind and reassuring just as if he had been returning a home-sick child to a boarding school. 'This is fine June, so comfortable, I think you are going to be really happy here and I'll show you how to turn on the TV.' Dear man, I remember finding it hard to swallow my tea, I had such a lump in my throat, and when he had left me, I felt awful, and I wanted to go home. I'll ring for a taxi tomorrow, I thought.

Walking into the restaurant for dinner on my own was hard, for all the other tables were taken by smiling family groups. But by the next morning I gave myself a firm talking to and looked again at the lovely arrangement of flowers that Davina and Richard had sent me. The rain had stopped, the sun had come out, and the seagulls were screaming with excitement on the roof outside my window. 'Get on with it, girl,' I could hear D tell me and I did. Jimmy had taken me to some lovely places, but we never had a really seaside holiday and Lyme Regis seemed the perfect place to be. It was not too big and very pretty and friendly, and I rediscovered the first heart lifting smell of the sea and seaweed, and I enjoyed looking around the little shops bursting with buckets and spades and postcards and fossils. I also found some quiet corners in the public gardens where I could sit and cry and mercifully no one could see and no one could hear.

Some days I took long walks down to the Cobb and all around the town on a guided historical tour and one day I went out on a mackerel fishing boat with a crowd of other holidaymakers. My swollen face went down and I began to feel better and looked at Lyme's strange limestone cliffs dating back some 205,000,000 years, with their treasure store of fossils, not so very long ago compared to the age of the earth. Life began to settle into perspective and I remembered a fellow guest browsing through the herbaceous border at the hotel: 'It's all so lovely dear and now we have the autumn to look forward to.'

2001 brought appalling worries to the countryside. Widespread flooding followed by the tragedy of foot and mouth that had such widespread effects on so many people's lives. But I was lucky, for just before Christmas I flew out to South Africa to spend a wonderfully happy holiday with Davina and Richard in their delightful little house, which they built at Somerset West near Cape Town. Vi and Henry were looking after the cottage and Sophie was staying with Liz and Richard.

Sophie seems to have crept into this saga without any introduction. When Vicky developed heart trouble after gorging herself on crab apples, Jimmy and I had discussed whether it would be wise to have another Labrador and we decided as long as it was laid down in our will who should love her and care for her, we would have one more. And Derrick Berridge very nobly agreed to give her basic training. We saw Sophie's half sister at a funeral and I lost my heart. She was so like Brock and I have always believed lighter bones are less likely to lead to arthritis and other worries in later life.

We found the breeders, a charming family in Dorset and by a miracle; their yellow Labrador produced four black girls. I was not worried about her pedigree for we had no intention of breeding or training her for shooting. But about a week after we collected her I did look at her pedigree and saw that it was one, which would have definitely startled D. On her father's side, every name was either a field trial champion or field trial winner except one poor chap. I wondered if he cried at cover. And on her mother's side they were all show winners including best puppy at Crufts. What really mattered was that Sophie herself would prove a precious last link in that chain of beloved animals, dogs, cats and horses, which had been our dear companions.

Sophie is beautiful and infinitely loving and she has a charming habit of curling up her lips in a smile for special friends. She sometimes crosses her paws, enjoys classical music, but frequently puts herself to bed in another room when the news comes on and who could blame her. But I must stick to my theme. I thought South

Africa was incredibly beautiful with its seacoast, mountains, massive flowering trees, and flowers and it was good to remember that my grandparents had been here about a century before; that D had loved Africa perhaps more than any other continent and that Jimmy had stayed here briefly on his way back to England during the war when he was still recovering from polio.

Davina and Richard and their two daughters and grandchildren really spoilt me. We wined, dined, played with the children, and drove all over the Western Cape. We went to the opera and the pantomime and took a boat trip round Cape Town harbour. We also saw a huge camp of immigrants, which was sad and depressing, but I gathered they were now able to get water and electricity, so things were improving slowly. Our communion service in the local church on Christmas day was very moving, for the congregation was made up of every possible colour of skin and one felt it was indeed a sign of peace, reconciliation and hope.

After three happy weeks, Davina and Richard took me to the airport for my return home. Fortunately, they did not stay to wave my plane away, because it never took off. The aircrew who had shown us to our seats and given us a glass of orange juice were looking increasingly worried and at one time they started to hammer the plane underneath. Although Jimmy and I had often believed in the saying 'Give it a sharp tap with the hammer', when we were working on the cottage, this time it did not fill me with confidence. However, some hours later they must have decided it was all too difficult, for we disembarked and were put up in hotels in Cape Town. I found myself at midnight on the twenty-ninth floor of a five star hotel with a breathtaking view of Cape Town harbour, which was quite an experience, and on the journey home we had an excellent view of the eclipse of the moon from the air.

On my return home I decided I was going to tie up as many loose ends as possible, as I knew Jimmy would have wished, and while I still had some puff to tackle the bottom drawer. I worked my way through the various drawers and cupboards in the cottage and I asked Pete to build me a new incinerator. Pete is a very old friend who has taken me under his wing since Stan died. He used to sit beside Jimmy in the choir and find his hymns for him and apart from being a beautiful craftsman; he is infinitely kind with a refreshing sense of humour. The summerhouse with its wild assortment of family papers had to be tackled. I had pushed the papers back into any available space when I finished my book *A Long Way From Tipperary* and in amongst Wellington's letters, and threatening letters from the IRA to my poor great-aunt I found Mummie's school hat band, which she had worn when she was head girl and head of games at St. George's Ascot before the first world war.

I remembered Jimmy's teaching and decided to send this memento back to the school and I had a charming telephone call from the headmistress. I also started two things, which would have astonished Jimmy who knew my limitations only too well. I started going to a yoga class, hoping it would help with my breathing and panic attacks, and I also joined a computer class. They were interesting experiences but not really me. The yoga class aimed to get me to stand on my head, which made me giddy and I admitted to my teacher that I felt like a duck set down in the corps de ballet for Swan Lake. And the computer class was really hard going because I did not own a computer and not wishing to own a computer, I tended to forget between one Friday and the next. I hoped it was good for my brain and I actually won some certificates but I felt it was rather a farce because my screen frequently displayed a strange creature shaped rather like a paperclip who rolled his eyes at me and I gathered this meant help.

Some eighteen months after Jimmy died, Davina lost her beloved husband Richard from cancer and this sorrow followed only six months after the death of her mother. I'm very fortunate having several sweet cousins on Mummie's side of the family but I think Davina and her brother David have been the closest to me as they have seen me through so much and I always regard them as the brother and sister I never had. And now that we have both been widowed my bond with Davina seems even closer for we not only share family memories but we have both had to face a new future on our own.

For some years, I have tried to help our small church in various ways such as washing the alter linen and arranging the flowers, but then one day it dawned on Meg and myself that every week the church was being cleaned by two women and one had a pacemaker. I suggested to Meg that we might follow Mummie's example in helping her village church and recruit teams to lighten the load. Putting a notice in the parish magazine was unlikely to bring about any response. The only thing was to go around, knock on doors, and appeal to people's better natures. It worked and we recruited eighty-five volunteers, which made it possible to have twelve teams, one per month with a team co-ordinator and six or seven members. Meg and I found we had to put a lot of thought into picking the teams. We tried to put friends together if possible and if there were the odd touchy individual, it was best to place them with a tactful team leader. It has worked now for about ten years.

One of the byproducts has been that it has brought people into the church who never thought of going. They might not attend a service but it was no longer a strange dark mysterious building. It was familiar and they got to know the dusty corners and could talk and laugh when they turned out the flower cupboard, which had not been touched for years. Since Peg died and Meg has now moved away from the village we have handed the project on to two other friends, but last year it occurred to me that with the horrendous quotas that all churches now have to pay, there was very little money left for extra so-called frills. We had a meeting in the cottage for all the team leaders, and it was decided that the most pressing need was for a new church fence. The old fence had partly disintegrated and in some place, it was non-existent.

Our small fourteen-century church was first built at the time of the Black Death. Originally it was thatched and it is delightfully simple, and small enough to be intimate and welcoming. One team leader came up with the excellent suggestion that a bridge lunch was a good way of raising money if it was held in someone's home and so it turned out to be. We had two parties and the church cleaners cooked and waited and washed up and organised a raffle. With the top-up from another fund we raised enough money for a new fence, a Persian carpet runner and three new doormats, which was all very exciting.

Last year, I saw the fulfilment of a very personal quest. It was always D's wish that as Jimmy and I had no children, all the pictures, furniture and personal treasures, which came from Lissenhall, the old home, should return to Ireland on our death to furnish a room in memory of the Carrol family. It had been a long quest with many disappointments along the way but thanks to the kindness and concern of friends I have come to know the Limerick Civic Trust who recently restored a beautiful Georgian house in Limerick. The Chairman and Director who are the kindest and most thoughtful of men have visited me, and last August I dispatched the first flight of family treasures to Ireland. I have kept the furniture for my lifetime but I have sent pictures, silver, metals, swords and Napoleon's brother's coat, which had been acquired by my great-great-grandfather after the battle of Vittoria. I also sent all the family papers with the family Bible.

Last November, I was invited to the great opening of the exhibition by the British Ambassador. We were a party of seven. Angela and Peter Swift who brought about the introduction to the Limerick Civic Trust, my dear friend and solicitor John Isherwood and his wife Anne and David and Davina. Apart from missing Jimmy and my parents who I knew would be so thrilled at this happy outcome, we all agreed we could not have had a happier weekend. From the moment we arrived, we were welcomed and feted and every moment was filled with laughter and happiness. But the family treasures had been arranged with great care and exquisite taste and they shone out from their red silk lined cases like children at a party. Look at us, aren't we pretty and we have come home!

I think the little personal touches moved me most. About three days before our party arrived, three elderly men set out in the rain to the ruins of Lissenhall. They were determined that June should have an apple from her old home. And so Denis climbed an apple tree, Brendan stood underneath to catch the apples in his hat and afterwards Hiram took the fruit home to his kitchen and cooked the most mouth-watering apple crumble for our celebration supper. Denis had then disappeared into the ruined cellars on his own mission and as it was getting extremely dark Hiram and Brendan were a little concerned. They decided to contact him on his mobile phone but they then realised that neither of them could remember the number. However, after telephoning their office in Limerick they were told the number and Denis was discovered unharmed and quite unrepentant having found a brick and an old cooking pot from the old home. These two items were displayed in their own silk lined case, which made it all very personal.

I had only one criticism to make. On the back wall of the display room, a beautifully mounted board announced *The Carrol Collection: The Story of an Irish Family* and there they all were – pictures of my great-great-grandfather, my great-grandfather, my grandfather and my father, all looking extremely handsome and distinguished and at the very end, an enlargement of a very homely snap of me. I told Denis I didn't want to be difficult and it was probably very good for my humility, but could I not send him an alternative picture? When

I discovered how much the display board had cost them, I told him to forget it, but I believe one day he is going to stick another photo of me over the top of the other.

After the pictures and swords had been sent to their new home, the walls of the dining room and stairs looked like a chequer board of faded patches. And so it was imperative to have them re-papered, and in August, kind John appeared with his paste and paint pots to give me a new start. I have discovered that decorating is addictive. And when we saw the dining room with its new coral gold coloured paper it was obvious everything else needed a new look too and I ended up re-decorating the whole of the ground floor, which had not been touched since Mummie died in 1984. At the time I wondered what I had started, when Sophie and I were faced with everything including the bottle of aspirin under dustsheets. But it was a wonderful chance to give everything an extra clean and dust. I would have shunned some tasks but Cinders would not have let me. And every piece of china and every picture had to be polished and washed.

Vi and Henry and Cinders have helped to hold us up for over thirty years. Vi with her nursing training was a marvellous support with Mummie and Jimmy's last illness. In fact, she was with us the night Mummie died. Like the best kind of nurse and nanny, she was never demoralised or put off by the inevitable accident but always calm and resourceful. She remained calm and uncomplaining when she lost the sight of one eye but apart from not seeing to sew she still comes to set me right every Wednesday morning. Both she and Henry have spiritual gifts of healing and Henry has the greenest of fingers and thumbs.

Lately I have been concerned that Henry was looking a little tired. He had Lymes disease a few years ago, caught from a tick in the New Forest, and a garden on two levels is not the easiest to control. But we now have Sue to help him. She is gentle, tactful, and pretty and she has undoubtedly improved Henry's morale. He has not spoken

The Carrol sundial at Rose Cottage.

of arthritis pains in some weeks and he almost skips up the garden path, confiding to me in a whisper. 'Nice little thing, quiet, does what she's told.' As for Cinders when she is not helping me in a hundred ways with the cottage, she gives her time voluntarily to helping run an old people's club. She used to be the school cook at Weyhill School where I taught, and she has now been a very good friend for at least thirty-three years. Apart from keeping the cottage shiny, she had helped me pack up and deliver my Christmas presents, packed me for Ireland and South Africa, helped me bath Sophie and set up my deep freeze with delicious meals.

Over the years we have all shared our sorrows, anxieties and laughter and I regard them as my extended family. There is one question I sometimes ask myself and I know I shall never find the answer. Why was I born to be me? Looking round our miraculous globe I know there are so many millions alive today who have a daily struggle to exist, who have to face poverty and pain and sometimes unbearable cruelty through no fault of their own. And yet for some mysterious reason, I was chosen to be one of the lucky ones with a beloved family, a comfortable home, the dearest of husbands, many lovely friends and thanks be to God, so far only minor aches and pains.

I know I do not deserve such good fortune, but I do thank God most humbly for his gifts, and pray I never take them for granted. I believe laughter and a sense of the ridiculous can ease a number of tensions, and it is vital to be able to laugh at one self. Tomorrow is another day and who knows what it may bring, but I pray I may be of some use to those around me and that I may continue to learn, being well aware that I knew so few of the answers.

When I was teaching Class II, I used to make them write down this little poem, which was quoted by King George VI in one of his Christmas broadcasts:

> *And I said to the man who stood at the gate of the year.*
> *'Give me a light that I may tread safely into the unknown'*
> *And he replied, 'Go forth into the darkness and put*
> *your hand into the hand of God. That shall be to you*
> *better than a light and safer than a known way.'*

~ END ~